MW01034199

"If you long to make choices th[...]
book. Instead of jumping from [...]
highest and holiest call on you[...]
in your daily decisions. *The Life You Crave* will give you a plan for
distinguishing the difference between better and best."

— CAROL KENT, speaker; author of *When I Lay My Isaac Down*

"Life is complicated. Making good decisions is essential. If the cry for
wisdom echoes through your soul, this is your book! With authenticity
and warmth, Jerusha leads readers to understand that the key to enjoying life and choosing well is embracing the promise of discernment."

— BECKY HARLING, author of *Finding Calm in Life's Chaos*
and *Rewriting your Emotional Script*

"Authentic, genuine, and heartfelt. This is Jerusha doing what she
does so well: asking tough questions and then helping you reason and
discern the answers so that you can live the life you crave."

— LORRAINE PINTUS, coauthor,
Intimate Issues and *Intimacy Ignited*

"Jerusha is a wonderful writer who understands that the core of our
being is a desire for an intimate relationship with God. In this book,
she teaches us how to discern God's will and grow deeper in our faith.
You will learn a great deal about developing a deeper relationship with
God."

— JIM BURNS, PhD, president, HomeWord; author of *Creating an
Intimate Marriage* and *Confident Parenting*

THE LIFE YOU
Crave

the promise of discernment

JERUSHA CLARK

NAVPRESS

OUR GUARANTEE TO YOU

For a free catalog
of NavPress books & Bible studies call
1-800-366-7788 (USA) or 1-800-839-4769 (Canada).
www.NavPress.com

ISBN-10: 1-60006-055-2
ISBN-13: 978-1-60006-055-7

Cover design by The DesignWorks Group, Charles Brock, www.thedesignworksgroup.com
Cover image by Getty Images
Creative Team: Rebekah Guzman, Kathy Mosier, Darla Hightower, Arvid Wallen, Kathy Guist

Some of the anecdotal illustrations in this book are true to life and are included with the permission of the persons involved. All other illustrations are composites of real situations, and any resemblance to people living or dead is coincidental.

Unless otherwise identified, all Scripture quotations in this publication are taken from *THE MESSAGE* (MSG). Copyright © 1993, 1994, 1995, 1996, 2000, 2001, 2002, 2005. Used by permission of NavPress Publishing Group. Other versions used include: *The Living Bible* (TLB), Copyright © 1971, used by permission of Tyndale House Publishers, Inc., Wheaton, IL 60189, all rights reserved; the *New Revised Standard Version* (NRSV), copyright © 1989, by the Division of Christian Education of the National Council of the Churches of Christ in the USA, used by permission, all rights reserved; *The Holy Bible, New Century Version* copyright © 1987, 1988, 1991 by Word Publishing, Dallas, Texas 75039. Used by permission; the *Good News Bible Today's English Version* (TEV), copyright © American Bible Society 1966, 1971, 1976; and the *Holy Bible, New Living Translation* (NLT), copyright © 1996. Used by permission of Tyndale House Publishers, Inc., Wheaton, Illinois 60189. All rights reserved.

Library of Congress Cataloging-in-Publication Data

Clark, Jerusha.
  The life you crave : the promise of discernment / Jerusha Clark.
    p. cm.
  Includes bibliographical references.
  ISBN 978-1-60006-055-7
  1. Discernment (Christian theology) I. Title.
BV4509.5.C5185 2008
248.4--dc22

                        2007038643

Printed in the United States of America

1 2 3 4 5 6 7 8 9 10 / 12 11 10 09 08

To Kathryn Hansen for modeling joy in mourning and to Kathy Moratto, who never settles. Thank you, dear friends, for helping me experience deeper and truer Life.

Contents

Acknowledgments

THIS BOOK SIMPLY WOULD not be without . . .

- The Source of all Truth and Goodness, Beauty and Hope: Yahweh, Jesus, Holy Spirit. I am Yours.
- My husband, Jeramy, whose faithful and fiery love continually uplifts me.
- My mother, LeAnn Redford, who edited brilliantly, prayed devotedly, and first taught me about discernment.
- My father, J. A. C. Redford, whose wisdom and love play a role in everything I write.
- My Brudi, Jonathan Redford, whom I cherish and adore (more than he knows).
- My brother, Ian James, whose zeal for Life is incomparable and inspiring.
- Spencer and Rona Clark, who encourage me continuously.
- The prayer team, whose loyal intercession sustains me.

- Aunt Penny and Uncle Tom, who give our family everything from Tuesday play dates to heart fellowship.
- Christine Hammill, whose intelligence and passion change lives.
- Cameron Germann, who courageously chooses to live what she learns.
- Janice Prince, whose obedience makes things happen.
- Lorraine Pintus, who really *knows* and *lives* and *loves*.
- Breanna McIntyre, whose affirming e-mails infuse me with fresh energy.
- Rebekah Guzman, who edited this project beautifully and wisely.
- Nicci Hubert, whose skill shaped these ideas at their earliest stages.
- Kathy Mosier, whom I always look forward to working with.
- The staff at RBBP — Nancy, Sandy, Betty, Mary Ann, Kristin, Tina, Carolyn and Keta — who lovingly cared for my daughters (and allowed me to invade their space too).

I am indebted to each of you. Thank you.

Foreword

Shannon Ethridge, M.A.
Best-selling Author & Speaker

I recently attended a fiction writer's conference in New York City, led by a gruff and intimidating sort of man who is considered a top expert in the field. The conference room was filled with 250 aspiring screenplay writers and fiction novelists, all of whom were soaking up every word and scribbling out a plethora of notes over the course of the three-day seminar.

At the beginning of each scheduled break, the speaker boldly warned, "You are welcome to approach me with your comments and questions about the material I've presented. *DO NOT, however, ask me what you should do in the particular story you are writing!* The answer is, 'I DON'T KNOW! You're the writer, so you figure it out!'"

While I was surprised by these warnings at first, I realized why it was necessary for the speaker to take this stance with us. He didn't want to derail our best creative efforts by speaking into a project he was completely unfamiliar with. How could he possibly be expected to know how to direct all 250 people with their individual manuscripts, other than just give us general instructions about the art of writing well? *After all*, I thought, *he's just a teacher. He's not God.*

But guess what? God *is* God! He is more than capable of directing our stories—the story of each of our lives. He's very familiar with our past, our present, and our future, so who better to offer us guidance in life than God? Although He gives us absolute freedom of choice and complete creative liberty to author whatever life we want for ourselves, He certainly stands ready and eager to guide us into the fulfilling life we crave. Aren't you glad God doesn't have a "you figure it out!" attitude with His people? I am!

We can't underestimate the value of God's free guidance because sometimes our cravings can deceive us. Our flesh cries out to be satisfied by certain things that ultimately leave us longing for more and more. None of us wants to be a slave to our own passions. Fortunately, the gift of God's discernment will show us how to get our needs met in such a way that we're master over our flesh, not vice versa. And in today's *"If it feels good do it!"* kind of world, such discernment can mean the difference between living an absolutely delightful lifestyle or an absolutely destructive lifestyle.

I get e-mails every day from women of all ages who, after reading *Every Young Woman's Battle* or *Every Woman's Battle*, ask questions such as, "How can I keep this relationship from becoming inappropriate?" or "If I've been having sex already, how can I stop?" or "How can I keep our love alive after all these years? How can I affair-proof our marriage?" Looking past the written words these women use to pose their questions, it's easy to recognize what they are *actually* asking. Just like most Christians on the planet, they are looking for discernment in how to make life work both to their advantage and to God's glory. If you are looking for the same thing—discernment in creating a lifestyle that is both pleasing to you and to God, you're holding the right book in your hands.

Although Jerusha and I have never met face-to-face, God certainly used her insightful writing to walk me through some pivotal decisions in my life. I found it so ironic (a.k.a. a "God-thing") that I was asked to review this manuscript during a season that my brain was overflowing with questions such as, *Should I try my hand at a fiction novel or stick with nonfiction? . . . Should I move forward with this particular conference date or should I postpone? . . . Should I try to lose a few pounds or just accept myself the way I am? . . . Should I apologize to this person for what I said or move on and hope they didn't take it the wrong way? . . . Should I pursue a higher level of education or just be content with the degree I have?*

Granted, none of these decisions were going to make or break my salvation. But like you, I always want to do the best thing, the right thing, the most God-honoring thing. I've already made the "biggest" right decision to surrender my life to Christ, but on a day-to-day, minute-to-minute basis, sometimes it's easy to lose sight of what making the best decisions looks like. That's why we all need to open God's gift of discernment each and every day, often several times a day.

But let me also give you a fair warning. If you're looking for someone to tell you what to do at every turn, or if you're searching for hard and fast rules about how to make every decision in life without ever blowing it, please consider this: no author could ever write that book. You can save yourself the trouble of searching for it!

However, if you're looking to establish a more intimate, fulfilling relationship with the God who deeply desires to help you author your own wonderful life worth living, then read on and get ready to mine the vast riches found in these pages!

Introduction

DO YOU WANT TO know God's will for your life?

I know I do, often desperately. There have been times when I've literally ached, longing to know what God would have me do.

As I think back on some of the major decisions I've made—where to go to college, what course of study or career to pursue, whom to marry, when to have kids (or even if I should)—I distinctly recall wishing, on more than one occasion, that God would send me a sign, making it absolutely clear what He willed for my life.

And I know I'm not alone in this. When churches offer Bible studies, when organizations offer seminars, or when books offer tips and techniques on "knowing the will of God," people respond eagerly. Why is it that even if twenty other choices are offered, half the people attending a conference sign up for the class on determining God's will?[1]

Nearly a hundred years ago, Christian scholar Evelyn Underhill answered this question brilliantly: "Men have three wants, which only God can satisfy. They need food, for they are weak and dependent.

They need forgiveness, for they are sinful. *They need guidance, for they are puzzled.*"[2]

While I might readily acknowledge that I need God's guidance, I'm not always keen to admit that I'm puzzled. Yet when confronted with life-changing choices, "puzzled" pretty accurately describes my state of mind and soul. And to be really honest, it's not just the big decisions that unnerve me. Sometimes the smaller, seemingly less significant choices I face day-to-day leave me perplexed and wondering, *God, what in the world do You want me to do?*

Because I'm often puzzled and need guidance, and because I want to know God's will not merely in the big things but also in the daily, sometimes mundane decisions, I decided to explore what it takes to make wise choices. This book grew out of that search.

Through the process of researching and writing, I've discovered that choosing to live in God's will is the most fulfilling and thrilling thing we can do; it allows us to live the life we crave. But to experience this, we need discernment.

I've also seen that my friends want direction. Though they often seek God on their own, they sometimes ask my advice as well. Indeed, many of the decisions we make over the course of a lifetime happen in community. When the people I love ask me to pray for them or give them counsel, I need discernment to speak God's truth and to encourage.

Discernment is one of those biblical-sounding words that Christians use when they pray ("Lord, please give me wisdom and discernment in this situation"). But how many people do you think *really* know what they're asking God to provide?

If you would've asked me to explain discernment a few years ago, I might've fumbled around a bit with words like *guidance* and *direction*. I probably could've produced an authoritative-sounding definition good enough to satisfy some of the students I work with. But I'm pretty certain I couldn't have convinced myself. Frankly, I just didn't under-stand what discernment is, let alone the role it plays in my life.

Yet as I mature in faith and as I come to grips with the labyrin-thine complexity of life, God continues to teach me about discern-ment. One of the most powerful lessons I've learned is that God gives us incredible freedom of choice. Of course, with this freedom comes great responsibility.

Some influential thinkers—existentialists and postmodernists in particular—believe that humans are lonely creatures, bearing the weight of a terrifying freedom to choose, yet finding themselves adrift in a world of meaninglessness.

We live in a world where such relativistic thought reigns. Many people view values and morals as purely human creations. For these people, ethics, commitments, and even religions enable mankind to survive with dignity in a meaningless world, but they are only privately constructed and relative truths.

Tragically, many Christians unwittingly go along with this world-view, relegating faith to the territory of subjective experience. In doing so, they, too, begin to see their freedom of choice as an alienating and often unbearable burden.

But we are *not* alone and adrift. Choice doesn't have to be a terrify-ing freedom. The moment we surrender our lives to God, He seals us with the Spirit, the Source of all wisdom and discernment. If we desire to live well, we can consistently attune ourselves to the voice of God's Spirit, who promises to direct us.

Sometimes, however, we fear choosing so much (perhaps because we don't want to make a "wrong" or "bad" choice) that we spend all our time and effort trying to follow systems or formulas. These programs and prescriptions are supposedly designed to help us decide, but what we actually hope is that they'll decide for us.

In his insightful book *Discernment: The Art of Choosing Well*, Pierre

Wolff wrote, "We [may be tempted] to believe that somewhere some-one has what we don't have, knows what we don't know, knows on our behalf. That is why we are ready to abdicate our responsibility and to submit ourselves to [people] we believe to be inspired."[3]

This is part of the reason we sign up for seminars and read books on "knowing God's will." We assume that the teacher or author must have some special insight we don't have. Oftentimes we hope they'll offer a step-by-step plan for determining what God wants us to do.

But we need not (and truly cannot) abandon our decision making to authority figures, abstract principles, or "surefire" formulas. There is a better way: the way of discernment.

As Paul wrote to the Corinthians two thousand years ago, I ask you,

> *Who ever knows what you're thinking and planning except you your-self? The same with God—except that he not only knows what he's thinking, but he lets us in on it. God offers a full report on the gifts of life and salvation that he is giving us. We don't have to rely on the world's guesses and opinions. We didn't learn this by reading books or going to school; we learned it from God, who taught us person-to-person through Jesus, and we're passing it on to you in the same firsthand, personal way. (1 Corinthians 2:11-13)*

What a radical, life-transforming thought: God teaches us *person-to-person*. We learn from God, who lets us in on what He's thinking. He doesn't want us to abandon our decision making to anyone but Him. Paul continued by exhorting the Corinthians,

> *Your life of faith is a response to God's power, not to some fancy mental or emotional footwork by me or anyone else.*
> *[Other people], of course, have plenty of wisdom to pass on*

to you once you get your feet on firm spiritual ground, but it's not popular wisdom. . . . God's wisdom is something mysterious that goes deep into the interior of his purposes. You don't find it lying around on the surface. It's not the latest message, but more like the oldest—what God determined as the way to bring out his best in us, long before we ever arrived on the scene. . . .

Spirit can be known only by spirit—God's Spirit and our spirits in open communion. Spiritually alive, we have access to everything God's Spirit is doing. . . . Isaiah's question, "Is there anyone around who knows God's Spirit, anyone who knows what he is doing?" has been answered: Christ knows, and we have Christ's Spirit. (verses 5-7,14-16)

Other people may have "plenty of wisdom to pass on"—and I pray that through the following chapters I might encourage you with some of what God has taught me—but this book cannot and will not give one-size-fits-all (or even one-size-fits-most) answers. Instead, I sincerely hope that God will allow us to journey together into His wisdom, the mysteries that go "deep into the interior of his purposes."

Long before any of us came into this world, God determined that the way to bring out His best in us was to give us the freedom to choose. He gave us a will and a spirit that could respond to His: "God's Spirit and our spirits in open communion."

This idea radicalizes how we look at determining God's will. Our good Father invites each of us to get below the surface, to look beyond the latest messages of gurus or savants. "Do not be conformed to this world," He proclaims, "but be transformed by the renewing of your minds, so that you may discern what is the will of God—what is good and acceptable and perfect" (Romans 12:2, NRSV).

So that *you may discern.* Not so that your pastor, parent, spouse, or spiritual director might determine God's will for you (though they certainly may be able to help you). So that *you* may discern.

Wouldn't it be great if you could actually distinguish on a regular basis — being taught person-to-person by Christ's Spirit within and around you — what God wants you to do and who He wants you to be?

You can!

Knowing God's will is not a special gift reserved for the ultra-holy, nor an otherworldly occupation that has little to do with everyday life. Jesus came to answer the most pressing questions of our very real, sometimes very difficult and complex, existence.

And what joy it brings to recognize that in doing so, Christ doesn't simply mete out a bearable existence. By no means. As author Dallas Willard so incisively observed, "Jesus came to respond to the universal human need to know how to *live well.*"[4]

We don't merely want to "do the right thing." We want to — rather, I would say we *need to* — live well. We crave the kind of life Paul asked God to give his beloved Ephesians:

> *I ask — ask the God of our Master, Jesus Christ, the God of glory — to make you intelligent and discerning in knowing him personally, your eyes focused and clear, so that you can see exactly what it is he is calling you to do, grasp the immensity of this glorious way of life he has for his followers, oh, the utter extravagance of his work in us who trust him — endless energy, boundless strength! (Ephesians 1:17-19)*

Would you read these words with me again, slowly savoring what God wants to give us? These verses are my prayer for you. I pray you would know God intimately and see with intelligent understanding and clear vision "exactly what it is he is calling you to do." I also pray that you would experience the vast and splendid way of life Jesus died to offer you.

I invite you to look at this book as the start of an adventurous dialogue between you and God. At the end of each chapter, you'll find questions that can be used for discussion in a small-group setting or as journal prompts. You'll also find some thoughts for personal meditation and a prayer to spark your conversation with God. I pray these exercises will take you deeper into the life of endless energy and boundless strength that God promises.

It's also my hope that you'll be encouraged to keep pursuing the open communion—Spirit to spirit—that God offers to *all* who want to know and do His will.

If you're hungry for a better life and if an intimate relationship with God is what you crave, the promise of discernment is yours. Are you ready to grab hold of it?

ONE

Discernment

THE ART OF LIVING WELL

WHEN I WAS GROWING UP, even good Christian girls were encouraged to live by a hodgepodge of pop culture slogans such as "I am woman; hear me roar," "Be all that you can be," and "You can do anything you set your mind to." Right or wrong, all of these boiled down in my mind to one message: You'll either be a stellar success or a complete failure; mediocrity isn't an option.

There was never any discussion as to whether or not I would go to college. In my family it was fully expected, and I had no reason to oppose or question this decision. I assumed God wanted every woman to get a degree and a job (at least until she got married), but I really never asked Him. Though I was a Christian, I barely stopped to pray, let alone consider whether my ambitions were true, beautiful, or good.

Getting into college was somewhat of an obsession for me. Supposedly, picking the "right" major and securing the "right" degree would answer all my questions about the future. Apparently, most people also meet their spouse during college.

But neither of these happened for me.

Studying—even at a great university—did *not* give me clear direction for my life. As is the experience of many others, my college years were filled with big questions instead: What should I do with my life? If I pursue a career, does that mean that marriage and kids will have to wait? If I get married, will that nullify my career plans? What if I never get married at all? What will my life look like then?

Those years exploded with thousands of smaller questions as well: Should I get involved with this activity or that? What church should I attend? What should I do with the free time I have? Who should I spend that time with?

And every day, I had to make decisions about specific issues that confronted me: Can I stay true to my faith and remain friends with my dance partner, Darrel, who announced his homosexuality on "National Coming-Out Day"? How do I respond to the catty girls who spread vicious rumors about me during first semester? My sex drive is starting to kick into overdrive; what do I do with that? Why do I hate my body?

As my faith matured, I became better equipped to answer questions like these. But let me be the first to admit I made tons of foolish choices during college. Until my senior year, I didn't have a framework for making good decisions. I prayed about things, but I didn't know how to genuinely listen for God's voice. If the Holy Spirit did speak to me, I wasn't even sure how to separate His voice from my own.

Feeling horribly conflicted one day, I remember grabbing my Bible in desperation and praying, *God, please speak to me.* I closed my eyes and opened the Scriptures, expecting that wherever I landed would be God's words for me that day. The crinkly pages opened to the book of Joel, chapter 3 if memory serves. I don't know how many of you have read Joel recently, but it's pretty intense. That day I found neither comfort nor direction for my confused soul.

Years later, I read an explanation of Christians who, in an effort to determine God's will, play games like "Bible roulette." This description so perfectly described my experience with the book of Joel that I laughed out loud and wanted to cry at the same time.

I really desired at that time to know God's will and direction. But it seemed so complicated. Though I may have prayed for "discernment" now and then, I didn't really understand that discernment was exactly what I needed.

And even though many of the questions of my college days have faded or been answered, I've seen other complex quandaries take their place. I still need discernment every day. We all do.

Because each stage of life overflows with decisions—whether big or little, general or specific, confusing and/or dangerous—we never stop needing discernment. Just because we figure out where to attend college, what to do for a living, or whom to marry does *not* mean we're done making tough choices.

But praying, *Please help me make the right decision*, and then going about business as usual doesn't work. It's certainly not enough to flip the Bible open to a random page. And it won't do us much good to ask for discernment if we don't know what it is.

That's why I'd like to take some time now to explore what discernment means and why practicing it enables us to live the lives we crave.

Life and Death, Blessings and Curses

For the single English word we translate "discernment," the Bible uses *eight* distinct terms—five Hebrew and three Greek. With this in mind, you can imagine the broad range of biblical applications for discernment.

In some instances, discernment simply means "to observe." However, it can also refer to understanding, wisdom, or common sense (as *The Living Bible* renders it); to insight and awareness; to perception and the ability to distinguish; to taste (as in "a discerning palette"); to the act of judging; to making distinctions, seeing clearly, showing prudence, paying close attention, or carefully, diligently, and intelligently considering.

Wow—that's a lot to take in!

But here's what brings it all together: Every biblical reference to discernment involves humans listening to God and using their minds, emotions, and senses to make wise decisions.

Even more important, the word *discernment* always implies a *kind of life*, a Spirit-filled way of thinking and acting that forms the fabric of an individual's life. Discernment is not a theory or a method as much as it is a way of life, a means of growing into the kind of people who habitually make good choices that enable them—and others—to live well.

Depending on how long you've been a Christian or what kind of mentoring you've had, you may have tried-and-true ways of dealing with big decisions. Perhaps you pray, search the Scriptures, ask the advice of godly friends, or engage in other spiritual disciplines.

And certainly these are all excellent ways to help determine the best course of action. But the reality is that we're often forced to make split-second decisions as well, spur-of-the-moment choices that affect our lives and the lives of others. What about those times when we have to act *now*, when we have no opportunity to read the Bible, pray for a couple of days, or ask for counsel?

As Gordon T. Smith said in *The Voice of Jesus*, "Our greatest need is not so much that we would learn guidelines to make the big decisions of life as that we would cultivate a context—a pattern of life, work and relationships—that is conducive to good decision making. . . . We need to foster an orientation of life that enables us to choose well."[1]

With God's help, we can develop this continual insight, this capacity to see clearly. We can learn to distinguish not merely between right and wrong but between good and better. And we can grow in the kind of knowledge and understanding that make sound judgment a routine expression of our character. This is what we call discernment.

Discernment can help us face the myriad challenges life throws at us. For instance, it can help us determine what to say to our close friends who tell us they're thinking about moving in together instead of getting married. When a loved one chooses an alternative lifestyle, discernment enables us to relate with gracious wisdom. It brings phrases like "love the sinner; hate the sin" into the realm of reality. And it helps us answer perplexing and ongoing questions, such as "How am I supposed to feel about sex or my body?" Discernment doesn't simply change the way we act or how we make decisions; it changes our very manner of thinking and being.

As the words of Deuteronomy 30:15-20 remind us, we need discernment because in every choice, God sets before us life and death, blessings or curses. I'm guessing you, like I, want to choose life and blessings. The problem is we don't always know how to do that; we're often drawn to death and curses, diabolically marketed as ways to better our lives. We need discernment to separate life from death, blessings from curses.

We find another significant reason for needing discernment in Psalm 119:125:

> Give discernment to me, your servant;
> > then I will understand your decrees. (NLT)

This shows that while the Bible is key in helping us make wise decisions, we require discernment even to understand God's Word.

And we need discernment because good intentions aren't always enough. It takes only a cursory glance at history to remind us that many claim they want to do the right thing but live deluded lives, harming themselves and others in the name of God. Even the most sincere and eager person can be led by misguided desires and motives masquerading as the will of God.

Clearly, we need discernment. But how do we grab hold of it?

Ask . . . Prepare . . . Practice

The poet of Psalm 119 acknowledged, "You, GOD, prescribed the right way to live." He declared with eager desire,

> *Oh, that my steps might be steady,*
> *   keeping to the course you set;*
> *Then I'd never have any regrets*
> *   in comparing my life with your counsel. (verses 5-6)*

I'd venture to guess that you'd like to look back on your life with no regrets. I'll bet you wish your steps could be steady, that you could keep the course God sets for you. Like this ancient poet, you probably know God's way is the "right way to live."

This led the psalmist, and should lead us, to *ask God* for discernment. We can also see, from Psalm 119:169, that the poet didn't merely ask—he requested that the Lord make good on His word as well:

> *O LORD, listen to my cry;*
> *   give me the discerning mind you promised. (NLT)*

In one way, it's so simple: To get discernment, we need to ask God. He pledges to transform our thinking, to make us discerning. And truly, His gracious offer is ours for the taking. To use our God-promised discernment *well* and *regularly*, however, requires preparation on our part. Though God gives discernment freely, it still requires something of us. As the book *Hearing God* notes, no "grace is . . . opposed to effort; it is opposed to earning."[2]

Grabbing hold of the life God provides and the discerning mind He promises does *not* mean abdicating our judgment. It never makes our decision-making process obsolete. On the contrary, as Jesus Himself proclaimed, "The way to life — to God! — is vigorous and requires your total attention" (Luke 13:24).

In his book *Renovation of the Heart*, Dallas Willard incisively observed,

> *We will not be able "on the spot" to do the good thing if our inner being is filled with all the thoughts, feelings, and habits that characterize the ruined soul. . . . The thoughts and feelings that the will depends on in any given moment of choice cannot be changed in that moment. But the will or heart can change the thoughts and feelings that are to be available to it in future choices.[3]*

A primary purpose of this book is to help us change the thoughts and feelings that will be available to us in future choices. No one can instantaneously overhaul their mind-set in a moment of decision. We can, however, prepare ourselves in advance to make good decisions. With practice, we can become people who discern *naturally* and *consistently*.

To start this process, we'll devote the remainder of this chapter to looking at general guidelines for discernment. In the chapters that follow, we'll apply these principles to specific areas of daily life. And in the benediction, you'll find some practical ways to exercise discernment in any situation.

Why Do You Want to Know God's Will?

It's imperative that we first explore—carefully, diligently, and candidly—what motivates us to ask God for direction. Genuinely longing to do God's will and "wanting God to help me" are distinctly different motivations.

Life experience teaches us that all humans share a common and often troubling anxiety about the future. Uncertainty haunts each of us to varying degrees; and at different stages of life, fearful doubts may threaten to consume us.

While there's nothing wrong with asking God to help us navigate the ambiguities of life, I find that people often want to hear from God solely to secure their own comfort, safety, and righteousness. Contrary to what people often believe, being preoccupied with "knowing God's will for me" sometimes indicates *self*-focused concern, not a genuine interest in God's glory.[4]

For instance, some people say they want to know God's will when really they want only to make decisions that are best for them. These individuals treat God's Word as a how-to book, a manual for getting out of sticky situations, staying out of trouble, or acquiring the kind of "good life" that our consumeristic culture glorifies. But living well doesn't automatically equal health, wealth, and worldly success.

Here's a challenging question for each of us to ponder: Do we genuinely want to know God's will, or do we merely want to know what decisions will make our lives as hassle-free as possible? Many people don't care to hear from God unless they're in trouble and need His help. But this attitude doesn't encourage authentic discernment.

Others, motivated by the desire for security and a doubt-free life, claim they want to know God's will, but what they really want is to be *right*. By focusing on external standards and reducing life to an orderly system of doing the "right things," some hope to preserve themselves from life's valleys—from confusion, doubt, and pain.[5] This often motivates perfectionists and legalists. Sadly, these impulses often drive me.

Sometimes legalists and perfectionists not only wish to avoid trouble but also want to know God's will ultimately so they won't have to depend on God. As Jerry Bridges revealed in *The Pursuit of Holiness*, many of us "cannot tolerate failure in our struggle with sin chiefly because we are success-oriented, not because we know it is offensive to God."[6]

Here's the problem: A trouble- or sin-free life on earth is strictly an illusion. Wanting to do the right thing so that we won't be inconvenienced and distressed or so that we'll succeed rather than fail doesn't prepare us to be people who make wise decisions consistently and naturally.

I like the way Martha Peace explored this idea in her book *Damsels in Distress*. She wrote, "Because of man's nature and his propensity to sin, he wants to make the Christian life workable in the flesh. The legalist looks for techniques and formulas (step one, step two) [because] commands are too general. He thinks he needs more organization concerning . . . the complexities of life. Some modern-day examples are 'steps to find God's will.'"[7]

We often listen to sermons, read books, and even study the Bible primarily because we want to make life work better. We hope to predict or control circumstances in an unruly and unmanageable world. Behind our alleged desire to know and do the will of God, we often find a stronger longing to escape the reality that we live in a broken world that isn't our eternal home.

But wanting to do the will of God cannot be a self-improvement project, one motivated by the desire for a better, easier, or less sinful life. If you want to live the life you crave, the life your soul cries out for, you're going to need more than a Christianity of tips and techniques.

Rather than a fixed blueprint or a closed script for life, God's will (the heart of Christian faith) is an *epic, vivid, and unfinished drama,* a story in which each one of us is invited to participate. Through our choices, our character either works with or fights against the grand narrative of God's eternal, creative design.

How different would life be if we all wanted to know and do God's will for *His* sake, if we desired that our life story influence a chaotic world for *His* glory? Then our choices would shape more than what we do; they would define who we are. We would become who God created us to be.

And isn't becoming everything God intended us to be what we *really* crave?

Renowned preacher E. Stanley Jones once observed,

> *The development of character, rather than direction in this, that, and the other matter, [is] the primary purpose of the Father. He will guide us, but he won't override us. . . . Suppose a parent would dictate to the child minutely everything he is to do during the day. The child would be stunted. . . . The parent must guide in such a manner, and to the degree, that autonomous character, capable of making right decisions for itself, is produced. God does the same.*[8]

What a life-altering thought: With respect to many choices in our future, God's will is that *we decide.* What we choose when not explicitly told what to do is the final indicator of who we are. What kind of person do you want your choices to reveal: someone who longs to know God's will for His sake or for your own?

Thought Life and Discernment

I know it can be painful to dig into our motives like this. Most of the time, we'd rather not evaluate why we do what we do. But as theologian J. I. Packer wrote in *Knowing God,* "To live wisely, you have to be clear-sighted and realistic—ruthlessly so—in looking at life as it is."[9]

A good deal of reality lies behind the scenes, where motives and underlying beliefs compel us to act. That's why, if we truly desire to live *well*, we must—with clear vision and ruthless realism—face our deepest thoughts and beliefs. The set of our mind determines how and why we act.

Over the past ten years, God has taken me on an amazing—though often heartbreaking—journey, deep into the corners of my mind. He has led me to consider the brokenness I've battled and still war against, and He has allowed me to share struggles that many women I love and admire also face.

Through experiences both painful and powerful, God has taught me that every act, whether beautiful or heinous, starts in the mind. Every inner conflict I've confronted can be traced back to a poisonous idea or set of ideas. And when I entertain toxic beliefs, my body and soul suffer. In contrast, when I dwell in and on Truth, my life reflects beauty and grace. Does this ring true for your life? For the lives of those you love?

In my book *Every Thought Captive: Battling the Toxic Beliefs That Separate Us from the Life We Crave*, I discuss this powerful truth: What we think determines what we do and say, which then determines who we are.

We tend to act as though what we're doing is more important than what's going on inside us. But our behavior is only a symptom of the true problem. If we want to choose well and *live well*, we have to get to the real root of our problems. We have to address our thought lives, the underlying beliefs that compel us to feel and act in certain ways.[10]

When I began researching for *The Life You Crave*, I never anticipated that I'd discover an intimate and foundational connection between thought life and discernment. Yet more and more clearly, I began to see that exploring discernment was a natural outgrowth of my original journey with God in "thinking about what we think about."

The Good News Bible renders Proverbs 4:23, "Be careful how you think; your life is shaped by your thoughts." Every decision we make starts with a thought, and day after day, woven from the string of a million miniscule choices, our beliefs determine the shape of our lives.

As Dallas Willard so wisely observed in *Renovation of the Heart*, "Thoughts are the place where we can and must begin to change. . . . The ultimate freedom we have as human beings is the power to select what we will allow or require our minds to dwell upon."[11] We can't always control what we're exposed to. We can't always determine what thoughts float through our mind. Try as we might, we can't control the outcome of every decision we make. But we *do* have the power and freedom to select what we'll set our minds on.

This God-given ability to determine the focus of our minds is one of the greatest and most indispensable freedoms we have. It is this power to choose what we'll think and believe about God, ourselves, and the world that enables us to discern consistently and well.

We can't make good choices about our bodies or sexuality, for instance, unless we live in Truth and not in lies. How we think about work and recreation, words and emotions, faith and the church makes a *tremendous* difference in how well we live. It changes how well we honor God.

In their devotional companion to *Renovation of the Heart*, Jan Johnson and Dallas Willard noted, "Bluntly, to serve God well we must think straight. Crooked thinking, unintentional or not, always favors evil. To take the information of the Scripture into a mind thinking straight under the direction and empowerment of the Holy Spirit is to place our feet solidly on the high road of . . . God."[12]

As we evaluate our motives and begin to think straight under the direction and empowerment of the Word and Spirit of God, we become better able to grasp the discerning mind God promises us. But for me and many others, this begs a question: What does it *really* mean to be under the direction and empowerment of the Bible and the Holy Spirit?

Mind Games

From childhood, we learn to determine the nature of things by recognizing their opposites—light and dark, wet and dry. In the same vein, I'd like to compare several common myths about being under the direction and empowerment of the Word and Spirit of God with their opposite . . . truth. Turning to less reliable—sometimes downright *false*—ways of discerning God's will can cause immense damage to our ability to make wise decisions. Abiding in Truth, however, enables us to live and choose well.

Below are some of the more prevalent misconceptions about how to determine God's will, contrasted by the truths that refute them:

- **The "Guess What I Want from You Now" Game.** Some people think God plays hide-and-seek with His purposes, concealing His will in a capricious "Ha! You want to know what to do, but I'm not going to tell you directly" fashion. This is neither the God Scripture reveals, nor a God we could lovingly serve. God's will may not be immediately clear. We may not completely understand all the hows and whys. But this doesn't mean God is hiding His will like the proverbial needle in a haystack. Otherwise the words of Psalm 143:10 could never ring true: "Teach me to do your will, for you are my God. Let your *good* spirit lead me on a level path" (NRSV, emphasis added). The Spirit is *good*, and He will teach us to do His will and lead us on a level path. God does not play mind games.

- **The "It Always Comes in the Same Way" Myth.** (a.k.a. "God's Guidance Comes Only Through One Source"—for example, prayer, the Bible, or a particular church). As *The Voice of Jesus* author Gordon T. Smith keenly pointed out,

  > We might miss the voice of Jesus because we are unwilling to hear him through the mode by which he is speaking. We reject what we are hearing and presume that this could not possibly be the voice of Jesus because of the source or the venue. However, a discerning person learns to be alert and attentive to the voice of Jesus in every context of life and, potentially, through unexpected channels of communication.

  Smith recalled that long ago, a hopeless sinner named Augustine was inspired to repent after overhearing the words of a child who was playing outside his window. What if Saint Augustine had pridefully assumed God could not speak through an "ignorant child"?[13] People are often fond of saying, "God works in mysterious ways," but few live as if it were true. Genuine discernment keeps us open to the surprises of God and the wonderful—if sometimes inexplicable—ways He chooses to encounter our minds.

- **The "Let's Just Pray About It" Fallacy.** While prayer is an essential component of wise decision making, the sentimentalized ideal that "all we need is prayer" can actually hinder our ability to hear from God. Discernment has little to do with "holy hunches" or attitudes that claim, "We don't need to be bothered with the facts; the only thing that matters is faith." As we just noted, answers don't always come in the form we anticipate, so the "prayer and nothing else" mind-set, which avoids evidence at hand and the way God speaks into the particularities of our lives, may lead to procrastination, poor decisions, or discouragement.

- **The "Whatever Happens Is God's Will" Illusion.** Believing that God is in control of everything, so whatever comes is from Him undermines our ability to genuinely discern. Not only does this fallacy wrongly deny the dynamic relationship between God and man, but it also fails to match up with our daily experience. For instance, it's absolutely true that God wants none "to be lost, but he wants all people to change their hearts and lives," as 2 Peter 3:9 (NCV) proclaims. But it's also true that many unrepentant people *do* perish. While we don't fully understand it (and I don't think we ever will comprehend this on earth), there is an authentic interplay between God, mankind, and the actions individual men take. Abdicating our decisions to a "whatever happens is His will" attitude can be very dangerous.

- **"It's All in the Bible" Thinking.** This is perhaps the most difficult and most important fallacy to expose, for it leads people to employ superstitious methods like Bible roulette (the "just flip the pages open" game I described earlier) or adhere to the idea that "every verse has something to say to me specifically and right now." Of course, God is big enough to use *anything*, no matter how misguided the approach used, to speak to a person genuinely seeking Him. But all ways of interacting with the Bible are not equally efficacious. In the words of Dallas Willard, the "it's all in the Bible" attitude

> *intends to honor the Bible, but it does so with a zeal that is not according to Knowledge. The Bible gives direct*

instructions about many situations in our lives. We do not
need to make long inquiries into God's will in order to know
whether we should worship an idol, take something that is
not ours, engage in illicit sex or mistreat our parents. But . . .
other questions force us to realize that many of the specific
circumstances of our lives are simply not dealt with in the
Bible. . . . The principles *are all there, however. I happily*
insist that so far as principles are concerned, the Bible says
all that needs to be said or can be said. But the principles
have to be applied before they can be lived out.[14]

It's discernment that helps us apply the principles of the
Bible. It's discernment that helps us determine how the stories
and rules of the Bible influence the concrete decisions we need
to make. For instance, we no longer exchange livestock as a
bridal price (see Genesis 34:12) or excommunicate someone
who touches his wife during her menstrual period (see Leviti-
cus 20:18). These were rules of *strategy* that enabled God's
people to live well in specific situations. But they are not meant
for everybody at all times. Discernment enables us to differentiate and to see clearly, especially when popular teachers claim
that certain portions of the Bible are out of date or have been
mistranslated. If we're to have any hope of navigating the battle
for what is true, we must learn to practically and consistently
exercise discernment when searching the Bible and applying it
to our lives.

Each of the methods just discussed is a false or incomplete way to
distinguish the will of God. But how, then, can we hope to hear God's
voice, to determine what He wants us to do? Now that we've looked at
a few of the ways God does *not* speak to individuals, let's look at some
of the ways He *does*.

How Personal Is Your "Personal Relationship"?

Christians often use the phrase "a personal relationship with Jesus Christ." At the same time, they sometimes express leery concern for the idea that individuals are created to hear God and develop an ongoing, conversational relationship with Him. But how can we possibly claim to have a personal walk with God unless we *can* and *do* have distinct, individual communication with Him?

We crave intimate and personal guidance. And this is exactly what God gives. He doesn't tell us the answers to all of life's questions in precise, biblical terms or formulaic step-by-steps. He intends for us to walk with Him *personally*. And a personal relationship with God includes guidance specific to the individual and changing circumstances of each disciple's life.

Spiritual writers through the ages have referred to "three lights," three ways God reveals His will to individuals: circumstances, impressions of the Spirit, and the Bible. We're all called to listen to God's voice and apply the Bible's general principles to our particular circumstances.

Most Christians agree that God wants people to use a biblical framework in making their decisions. But the Bible doesn't just tell us "the right thing to do"; it also beckons us to become players in the cosmic battle between Life and death, the battle present in each of our choices. Seizing this role requires listening to the impressions of the Spirit.

Now, I recognize that this phrase "impressions of the Spirit" may strike some people as a bit nebulous, possibly risky. The central question always seems to be this: How are we to tell if it's the Spirit impressing on our heart and mind or if it's something else doing it — our own thoughts or, worse, the slings and arrows of the Enemy?

This is a vitally important question and one that the Bible addresses. In John 10, Jesus declares, "The sheep listen to the voice of the shepherd.

He calls his own sheep by name and leads them out. . . . He goes ahead of them, and they follow him because they know his voice. But they will never follow a stranger. They will run away from him because they don't know his voice" (verses 3-5, NCV). John 10:6 says that when "Jesus told the people this story . . . they did not understand what it meant" (NCV). How I praise God that today we *can* know His meaning.

Psalm 95:7 clearly communicates, "We are his sheep, and he is our Shepherd" (TLB). This passage helps us understand that we are the sheep described in John 10, the sheep who can "know his voice." Jesus, our Good Shepherd, promises to call us by name (again, personally and individually). He also assures us that if something else (the Enemy or our own sinful hearts) tries to mislead us, we *will* be able to tell.

But let me explain this a bit further, lest some of you despair. Please don't believe this lie: "Maybe others can tell, but I've been dead wrong more often than not."

Humans recognize voices after prolonged exposure to them. How amazing it is that both of my daughters knew my voice at birth. When their tiny heads turned to hear me speak, the long months of carrying Jocelyn and Jasmine seemed worth every moment. Sometimes, however, it takes far less than nine months to recognize someone's voice. Though I've known her only a short time, the tenor of my girlfriend Sandy's unique voice makes it instantly identifiable.

In a similar fashion, we become attuned to the voice of God by continually focusing on its distinct character. I like how E. Stanley Jones described the distinguishing quality of God's voice: "The voice of the subconscious argues with you, tries to convince you; but the inner voice of God does not argue, does not try to convince you. It just speaks, and it is self-authenticating."[15]

Because consistent and close contact with His voice helps us to better recognize it, regularly immersing ourselves in the written Word of God is absolutely indispensable for living and choosing well. As we noted earlier, the Bible isn't the *only* way God speaks to us, but through careful listening to God's voice as revealed in Scripture, we can become better able to separate His communications from any other. Frederick B. Meyer, author of *The Secret of Guidance*, wrote, "The Word is the wire along which the voice of God will certainly come to you if the heart is hushed and the attention fixed."[16]

Here's the problem: Many of us fail to invest time and energy in learning to recognize God's voice. Some of us read the Bible to check one more thing off our to-do list or because "we're supposed to." But reading the Word in this way short-circuits the wire along which the Spirit of Truth speaks.

As we learn to more regularly hear God's Word through the Bible, we also begin to sense His personal direction for us in other ways. The impressions of the Spirit can then come to us in meditation and prayer.

Again, however, this takes time and energy. But let me pass along some exceptional (and simple!) advice I read in Dallas Willard's *Hearing God*: Start by setting aside a short time each day for silent meditation. By maintaining this consistent pattern of active listening, we become better equipped to more patiently, confidently, and accurately discern God's voice when we need particular direction from Him.[17] Though we might rush to God for answers when we're perplexed or in need of specific counsel, we can best hear His voice if we've developed the *general habit* of listening for God to speak during more peaceful times.

Imagine what our lives would look like if every day we laid our schedule before the Spirit, asking Him to direct our priorities for the hours ahead. Clearly, if we'd not taken the time to identify His voice, this would be a pointless and frustrating exercise. But I wonder what God would reveal to those who had chosen to discern His voice and heed it. I also wonder what He'd say to those determined to disobey.

Close observation of personal relationships indicates that recognition of certain voices can actually cue people to stop listening or can distort the message in a particular way, relevant to their unique interaction.[18] I wouldn't be surprised if this is what happens when God speaks to those in direct rebellion. Instead of prompting them to follow and *live*, His voice "cues" them to tune out or twist the message.

This brings to mind a story of two college students my husband and I knew. After dating for some time, the couple began to struggle with physical purity. They told us through tears that they had decided to pray, asking God if it was okay that they have sex. They were engaged, so it was just a matter of timing, right? They knelt down, bowed their heads, and "got the feeling" that God was fine with their decision either way.

They claimed they didn't hear from God that they *shouldn't* have sex. But the truth is they were willfully ignoring the fact that He *had* spoken this truth to them—and to all people—long ago. God clearly communicates through His Word: "Let marriage be held in honor by all, and let the marriage bed be kept undefiled; for God will judge fornicators [those who engage in sexual sin before marriage] and adulterers [those who engage in sexual sin outside marriage]" (Hebrews 13:4, NRSV).

I think what Dallas Willard noted in *Hearing God* likely came into play here: "Perhaps we do not hear [God's] voice because we do not expect to hear it. Then again, perhaps we do not expect it because we know that we fully intend to run our lives on our own and have never seriously considered anything else. The voice of God would therefore be an unwelcome intrusion into our plans."[19]

While these two young people believed they tried to listen to the impressions of the Spirit, they didn't simultaneously attune themselves to God's voice through the Bible or through their circumstances (the plain fact that they weren't married). Ignoring one or more of the three lights to focus only on one is treacherous indeed. In the *balance* of watching, listening, and meditating we find God's voice clearly directing us.

But what about the times we're not purposefully tuning God out yet still don't or can't hear His voice? Does not hearing from God automatically mean that we're living in sin or that we misunderstood Him at some earlier time?

As the apostle Paul might say, "By no means!" Let's look at what happens when we incline our hearts to the three lights but feel opposed or hear nothing.

Suffering Soldiers

The conflict-laden language of the Bible often unnerves people, even "good Christians." Many of us would like to ignore the sometimes fierce and bloody vocabulary describing God engaged in cosmic war. We don't like to acknowledge that there's a very real, wickedly cunning Enemy in this battle.

But all good stories reflect the epic story of God, the story of Life and death in vicious combat. The literature and movies that inspire us have a villain because our story has a villain. And this Adversary refuses to accept settlements. He seeks our complete annihilation, waging war to the death. He will oppose in some way—whether blatantly or nearly indiscernibly—every movement toward Truth, Goodness, and Beauty.

In John 10:10, Jesus plainly informed us that the thieving villain comes to steal, kill, and destroy. Why, then, do we continue to live as if he doesn't *actually* steal, kill, and destroy? It's time to wake up! Part of the reason we can't make good decisions is because we're constantly at war with an Enemy who plots our extermination and wishes our alienation from God.

The first attack our Adversary launched against humanity was a lie. He deceived Adam and Eve into believing that the "good life" could be found apart from God. His strategy has not changed since the Garden of Eden. He's still lying to people everywhere in the world, telling them that the life they crave and obedience to God's will are mutually exclusive.[20]

Our movement toward discernment, toward living and choosing well, angers the Enemy. He will try at all costs to undermine our trust in and ability to hear the Good Shepherd, who promises, "I came so they can have real and eternal life, more and better life than they ever dreamed of" (John 10:10).

Discernment helps us recognize that spiritual warfare is incredibly *personal*. A small portion of the cosmic fight is yours alone. We often think of the battle between heaven and hell in general or theological terms, but the supernatural conflict surrounding us affects our individual lives.

As Bible translator J. B. Phillips once wrote,

> *When a man becomes a committed Christian, . . . beneath the surface of things as they seem to be, he can discern a kind of cosmic conflict in which he is now personally and consciously involved. He has ceased to be a spectator or a commentator and a certain small part of the battlefield is his alone. He also becomes aware . . . of the forces ranged against him.*[21]

Discernment allows us to see beneath the surface of things, embrace the charge to fight the good fight, and courageously face the forces arrayed against us. When we feel our decision making opposed, when we feel in conflict, we can and — if we are to live the lives we crave — truly *must* take up the weapons of war.

Ephesians 6:10-18 and 2 Corinthians 10:1-6 describe the armaments God provides for us. These are divinely powerful weapons for destroying the Devil's strongholds (see 2 Corinthians 10:4). Some people feel discouraged by the spiritual nature of our armor. But the fact that our weapons are spiritual does *not* mean they are out of our reach. Just as our Enemy is real and fierce and our God is alive and almighty, the weaponry at our disposal is genuine and prevailing.

Meditate on the words of Ephesians 6:14-18. I strongly recommend memorizing these verses. Just as a soldier trains with his weapons in times of peace so that he can wield them effectively in hand-to-hand combat, become familiar with your armor. Ask God to equip you to handle it well.

Spiritual warfare can quiet God's voice in our minds and hearts. But as we learn to battle, we can fight to hear our Lord. Cosmic war, however, isn't the only force that threatens to silence God's voice. There's another kind of opposition that afflicts the army of God, one which calls us not to the frontlines of spiritual combat but to the valley of suffering.

As I noted before, many people want to know the will of God so they can avoid pain and confusion. But no matter how good the decisions we make, God never promises to remove us from the brokenness of our world. In *The Cry of the Soul*, Drs. Dan Allender and Tremper Longman pointed out this beautiful irony of the Cross: God overturned pain not by escaping it but by *experiencing it*. "We, too," they write, "encounter divine goodness in the midst of pain."[22]

In the Cross-centered life, suffering becomes part of God's loving and passionate engagement with wounded people, weaning us away from the fleeting and bonding us more completely with the Eternal. If we will courageously lean into the pain, we *can* discern the voice of Jesus coming through even the bleakest circumstances.

People often mistakenly believe, however, that though God allows suffering in Christians' lives, it's usually temporary and always teaches a clear lesson. There is some truth in both of these beliefs. Our suffering is temporary in light of eternity, and God does use every situation to make us more like Jesus. As Romans 8:28 proclaims, "That's why we can be so sure that every detail in our lives of love for God is worked into something good." But some take these truths and develop overly simplistic views of suffering, leaving people desperately trying to discern what they're supposed to learn from their father's cancer or their own financial ruin. In trying so hard to learn from our suffering, we sometimes focus more on our problems than on God.

The Old Testament, however, records a visceral account that reminds us that fixing our eyes on God is the *only* way out of suffering. Numbers 21:5-9 chronicles the story of God's chosen people:

> *The people spoke against God and against Moses. . . . The* LORD *sent poisonous serpents among the people, and they bit the people, so that many Israelites died. . . . Moses prayed for the people. And the* LORD *said to Moses, "Make a poisonous serpent, and set it on a pole; and everyone who is bitten shall look at it and live." So Moses made a serpent of bronze, and put it upon a pole; and whenever a serpent bit someone, that person would look at the serpent of bronze and live.* (NRSV)

Phyllis Tickle's brilliant words from *The Shaping of a Life* explain how this story helps us discern the mysterious and powerful ways suffering can lead us to engage more passionately with God than with our problems. Tickle wrote,

> *Those men and women and children who believed [Moses] and believed in Yahweh's message through him . . . looked up at the pole with its burnished snake and not down at the desert vipers who were besieging them. They elected by a combined act of will and faith to look, not down where the agony was and where the snakes might still be pulled from their bodies and their children's bodies, but up where the mercy was promised. They elected to be bitten in order that by faith they might live. I [have] lived long enough to know for a hard, enduring fact that*

life is full of snakes; that they bite fiercely; that they will kill you if you look down and wrestle them; and that, peculiarly enough, the very act of being wrestled with often is what gives them their potency. I [have] also learned that, just as the story teaches, looking up doesn't stop the pain immediately but it does prevent death from it.[23]

Oh how prone I am to look down at the serpents that encircle me, the sufferings that threaten my comfortable existence. It's extraordinarily difficult to *choose* to let myself be bitten. It's almost more challenging for me to imagine allowing my children to be besieged by suffering, even if it is only through it that we might really live.

But I, like Tickle, have lived long enough to know that life is full of snakes, and their venomous bites will kill. If I battle the reality that I and the people I love will be bitten, I will surely perish. Wrestling with the snakes, instead of with God (as Jacob did in Genesis 32:22-32), is a choice that moves me toward death, not toward the life I crave.

I've also seen that even if turning my eyes to the Son of Man lifted up "just as Moses lifted up the snake in the desert" (John 3:14, NCV) doesn't take the pain away, it does remove the sting of death from my suffering. Death has no victory over me when I choose Life.

As we fix our eyes on God, rather than on our problems, we can sense His voice coming through our suffering. It may not happen immediately; it may not happen in the manner we would choose. But the Lord vows to defend, protect, and preserve us. His promises extend to all who will choose Life. His promises are for *you*, and they open the door to what your heart craves most.

Questions for Discussion

1. Review as a group or ponder on your own (perhaps in a journal) the various reasons people want to know the will of God. What compels you to seek His will? What role do motives and intentions

play in making wise decisions? What about underlying beliefs and thoughts? Do you agree that thinking about what you think about is an important first step toward good discernment and the life you crave? Why is it difficult to get to the root of what actually drives us to make choices, whether good or bad?

2. In listening for God's voice, which method (as outlined on pages 35–38) trips you up the most? Did any of the methods identified as false or incomplete surprise you? Do you disagree with any of the ideas presented? Why?

3. What do you think about this chapter's discussion of spiritual warfare and suffering? Does it ring true with your own experience or the experiences of others you know? Why or why not? Read Philippians 1:29: "There's far more to this life than trusting in Christ. There's also suffering for him. And the suffering is as much a gift as the trusting." Talk to God (and your group) about any thoughts and/or feelings that arise while contemplating this verse.

Thoughts for Personal Meditation

How difficult is it for you to trust in the goodness of God and to actually live out the belief that if He wants you to know or do something, He will find a way to communicate it to you? Do you ever fear that you won't be able to discern whether it's God speaking to you or someone/something else? Do you ever tune out God's voice? Why? What did this chapter teach regarding these concerns? Review John 10:1-10. How can you incorporate a solid and practical trust in Jesus' words into your everyday life? Spend some time investigating this with the Holy Spirit.

A Prayer to Spark Your Conversation with God

Blessed be Your Name, O God, forever and ever. You know all and do all: You change the seasons and guide history, providing both intelligence and discernment. You make known secrets that are deep and hidden; You know what is hidden in darkness, and light is all around You. I thank You and praise You, God. Please give discernment to me, Your servant; then I will understand Your laws. Lord, listen to my cry; give me the discerning mind You promised.[24]

MORE (212) 541-6300
INFO (718) 290-2000
CALL (718) 297-7475

TWO

Emotional Discernment

FINDING THE STILL POINT

I'D LIKE TO SHARE a story with you about a woman who is eager to love and serve God but has learned some tough and significant lessons about emotional discernment. Here are her words:

> When I was in my twenties, more than anything else, I wanted to get married. But I'd heard that single Christians weren't supposed to obsess about marriage. So I spent hours trying to not think about what it would be like to be married. I wasn't terribly successful at this.
>
> I did find, however, that the more time I spent with God, the less concerned I felt about my singleness. My gnawing hunger for intimacy and love didn't go away, but the anxious wondering—will I ever experience fulfillment for these desires?—did subside.
>
> For several months, I spent an hour a day reading the Bible, praying, and devouring inspirational books. How fast those hours

with God seemed to fly, and how amazing He could make me feel. He cradled me in arms of love and nurtured me daily.

During this period, I also got involved with a ministry at the junior high school where I taught. I loved being able to tell the same kids I wrestled with over homework what actually mattered most to me — Jesus Christ.

Joel (not his real name, of course) worked with the parachurch organization in charge of weekly activities on our campus. He was fun and on fire for God and was everything I hoped for in a husband.

But remember, I was trying not to think about marriage. So I refused to pray about my growing feelings for him, secretly hoping that God would notice how "good" I was being at not making things happen on my own.

One Saturday morning, after a particularly awesome time with God, I hopped in the shower. As the hot water cascaded over me, I sang praise songs in my head and continued praying about things on my mind. Joel wasn't among them.

All of a sudden, seemingly out of nowhere, I had this picture in my mind: I was standing outside the doors to our church sanctuary, wearing a wedding dress. "Pachelbel's Canon" slowly floated through the air, and the doors opened. At the end of the aisle, smiling right at me, stood Joel.

Part of me couldn't believe it, and the other (much bigger) part of me thought, I knew it; this is it! God's showing me what's going to happen in the future. I was intoxicated and thrilled and absolutely captivated.

Naively, I assumed that because I'd been so intimately in Jesus' presence moments before, these thoughts had to be of God. Or maybe I just wanted them to be of Him so much that I didn't care to ask. I don't know exactly what I was thinking or choosing not to think. And I may never be able to know that.

But here's what I do know: This emotional experience drove most of my decisions over the next few years. Even when evidence contradicted my feelings, I trusted more in this "vision" than virtually anything else. For instance, Joel didn't show any particular interest in me, but I didn't let that get me down. I was convinced that God would bring us together; it was only a matter of time. I turned down dates with other men and steadfastly waited for Joel.

Some time later, the parachurch Joel worked with sent another staff member to our school. As cute as Laurel was, I never saw her as a threat. How could she be? I knew "from God" that Joel would be my husband.

But at our end-of-the-year party, more than a year after my "shower experience," Joel and Laurel acted really strange. They said they had a special announcement. I had no clue they were already engaged.

The confusion and betrayal I felt would be impossible to express. Anger and pain fought for my heart and fused into a toxic combination. No one knew about my shower experience, so I felt incredibly alone and afraid. Impulsively (and now I can say ridiculously), I resigned from my job and decided to move.

I also determined to silence my heart.

For the next three years I lived a numb, disengaged existence. People might well have described me as "cold" and "unfeeling." That was how I lived. Emotions were like a horrible affliction to me.

How strange and surprising it seemed when God started to thaw the ice on my heart. He allowed me to see how my choices — chief among them my attempt to live "emotion free" — spread devastating and far-reaching consequences through my life.

For some Christians, it would be easy to read my account and think, This just goes to prove that the heart is desperately wicked. You can never trust your feelings. But slowly, almost *imperceptibly, Jesus used the psalms and the writings of Christians across the ages to show me that the emotions I felt were not to blame. I shouldn't have completely disregarded the emotional experience I had nor given it the incredible significance that I did.*

Instead, this would have been a better course: weighing my feelings carefully in the light of godly counsel and God's Word, allowing the Lord to get to the root of what my feelings communicated, and then making decisions based on what came out of that journey. What I needed was discernment.

Stirrings and Storms

My friend's experience ran the gamut between giving emotions total control and trying to ignore them altogether. I, too, have battled with these extremes. Both of us have discovered that when it comes to emotions, discernment is key.

I come from a long line of extraordinarily passionate people. Feelings often ran hot and high in our home, and with six dramatically expressive individuals under one roof, you can well imagine the intensity of my childhood experience with emotions—and their power.

As I grew up, my dad repeatedly used two phrases about emotions. Both used to annoy me to *no end*. One came in the form of counsel: "Never make a decision at high tide." The other took the form of proverbial wisdom: "Not every feeling is valid."

During adolescence and a good deal of my early twenties, the idea that I should wait until the storm of emotion passed before making any decision struck me as frustratingly impossible. Life seemed at a perpetual high tide; college applications and deciding on a major, dating or wondering why I wasn't married yet, trying to figure out what an adult faith looked like and what I should do with my life were not low-tide matters to me. I often *had* to make choices in the midst of relative chaos. Now, having experienced a lot more of life than I had at fifteen or even twenty-five, I see the incredible importance of my dad's advice. I've learned that I can choose to stay at an emotional low tide, even when circumstances are pressurized and demanding.

It took me longer to figure out what Dad's other stock phrase — "not every feeling is valid" — meant. For years, I misunderstood why he said this to counsel me against making heavily emotionalized decisions. I assumed he believed that I shouldn't (in fact, that no one should) have certain emotions, that they were bad or off-limits. But this couldn't have been further from the truth.

If I'd taken the time to ask my dad what he intended to communicate, I would've discovered long ago that "not every feeling is valid" is an indispensable truth for living well. Why? Because it boldly recognizes the place of will and decision — the essential significance of discernment — in emotions.

For instance, I cannot always control whether I feel angry or fearful or zealously on fire. Sometimes physical and emotional responses arise despite my best intentions to keep a cool head. But what I *can* always choose is whether or not to validate these feelings.

Webster's dictionary defines the adjective *valid* with the following words: "sound; just; well-founded; authoritative." Similarly, *to validate* something involves giving "official sanction, confirmation or approval to" it.[1] Not every feeling is valid because not every emotion is either authoritative (able to appropriately control or direct a situation) or worthy of approval.

Some feelings can be dismissed almost immediately, not because it's wrong to have them but because to give them too much "playtime" would be to seriously misdirect ourselves. We can feel something but decide not to validate it. Other emotions need more time and testing. These feelings call us to evaluate whether they are well founded, just, and true. Exercising this faculty may take concerted effort at first, but with consistent practice it becomes easier to distinguish between the feelings that can be validated and those that should be disregarded.

Though we might like to, we can neither deny our emotions completely nor recklessly abandon ourselves to them. Because of this, I'd like to spend a few moments talking about the general and integral role of feelings in the Christian life. Then we'll get to the specific ways emotions and discernment intersect.

A Complicated Gift

Emotions are simultaneously one of God's greatest gifts and the trigger of our most pressing problems. Feelings can give us the thrill of being alive or make us wish for death. All that we see, all that we experience, all that we think can translate into feelings that move or paralyze us. The Bible explores this truth about emotions with honesty and intensity.

Solomon experienced emotional extremes. In Song of Songs 7:5 he wrote,

> *The feelings I get when I see the high mountain ranges*
> *— stirrings of desire, longings for the heights —*
> *Remind me of you.*

But in Ecclesiastes 4:2-3 he expressed, "I concluded that the dead are better off than the living. And most fortunate of all are those who were never born" (NLT). The rapturous sensations of love Solomon described in Song of Songs contrast starkly with the emotional apathy and despair that characterize much of Ecclesiastes.

In the same way, the transparent and raw feelings conveyed through the poetry of Psalms inspire us but often unnerve us simultaneously. Of the 150 poems in this book, a significant majority express the melodies of lament and accusation, confusion and doubt, heartbreak and anger.

Though deep-seated faith and joyful trust in the Almighty permeate even the darker passages, nearly every one of man's unrefined and painful emotions finds expression in the psalms.

The psalms vividly remind us that feelings play a central and extraordinarily important role in our lives. In fact, we rarely make a decision—no matter how minor—without some emotion attached to it. Even the "I don't care" apathy plaguing many in today's world doesn't reflect a true absence of emotion but rather a *determined choice* to feel little, a fixed decision to operate with a low-level (often angry) ambivalence toward life.

Involving our emotions when we make decisions is right and good and the way God intended us to function. Elohim, our wise and loving Creator, could have fashioned us without the capacity to feel. But in His goodness, He gave us hearts that could love, minds that could be stirred, and the charge to deal with our emotions responsibly.

God never intended, however, that we rely solely on our feelings when making decisions. This is the way of the worldly, who listen either to the "It doesn't matter anyway" apathy I described previously or to the "Follow your heart" messages perpetually pushed by the media.

As is true of a great deal of life in the Spirit, Christians find that a tension exists between two opposing forces, either of which taken to the extreme could utterly destroy us. We can neither deny our feelings nor give way to them entirely.

People sometimes use these words from Jeremiah 17:9 to brand emotions as dangerous and desperately wicked:

The heart is hopelessly dark and deceitful,
a puzzle that no one can figure out.

But this is both unbiblical and a life sentence for frustrated confusion. As you may have heard before, the biblical term *heart* does *not* refer strictly to the seat of human feelings. In fact, the Bible often uses *heart* synonymously with *mind* and *spirit*. Yes, the heart is the source of emotion, but it is also described as the center of thought, perception, and will.

When Jeremiah affirms the hopeless darkness of the human heart, he does so not to counsel God's people to focus on the imminent threat of their hearts. Rather, as *the very next verse* proclaims, Jeremiah calls us to focus on God; He alone can make sense of all our hearts communicate. Read verse 10 with me:

> I, GOD, search the heart
>> and examine the mind.
> I get to the heart of the human.
>> I get to the root of things.
> I treat them as they really are,
>> not as they pretend to be.

Why do we never hear this verse read in conjunction with the overused and misunderstood one that precedes it?

This passage of Scripture urges us not to focus on curtailing our "wayward hearts" but rather to let God get to the root of things, to travel with Him to the depths of our hearts. There our emotions and thoughts reveal what we think about Him, ourselves, and the world around us. He treats us as we really are (full of feelings) not as Christians sometimes pretend to be (free of or above feelings).

The pretense that emotions either don't really matter or should be ignored is a tragedy of modern evangelicalism. Old adages like "Our faith rests on the promises of God's Word, not feelings" can be both true and misleading. A diagram shown to many young Christians of a train with three cars, the engine labeled "facts," the middle car "faith," and the caboose "feelings" can similarly instruct or deceive us. In the wise words of *The Voice of Jesus* author Gordon T. Smith, this is "a woefully inadequate portrayal of the place of emotion in Christian experience."[2] Philosophers across the ages—whether believing or atheistic—have recognized that a difficult, complex, and *very real* relationship exists between reason and emotion. The train model disregards this important reality, probably because it cannot be neatly packaged.

A lot of Christians wonder, like I once did, *Does a train even need a caboose?* Some think that feelings are cute and fun but not necessary—a "bonus" for faith. And although who God actually is and what He actually says must remain more important than how we feel about Him or about a particular passage of Scripture, this does *not* make our emotions incidental to faith.

Images like the train often communicate the underlying and sinister perspective that feelings are a threat to true faith, not to be trusted and certainly an unreliable indicator of the character of our souls. This, however, simply doesn't reconcile with the whole of Scripture. It's not that I think we should rearrange the cars on the train. Emotions shouldn't be the engine or the middle car either. Perhaps we should chuck the analogy altogether and try for something that expresses the tensions we *know* exist between faith and feeling.

Where would we be without emotions that give weight and color to our convictions? What would it be like to acknowledge that we love God without feeling it? How sterile would the life of faith be without our emotional response to the true and good and beautiful?

Great Christian thinkers like Saint Ignatius, John Wesley, and Jonathan Edwards investigated and affirmed the role of emotion in the Christian life. Ignatius attempted to convince readers that without learning to take their feelings seriously, they could not know themselves or God. For Ignatius, attending to emotional dispositions gives Christians a key indicator of the work of God in their lives.

John Wesley made his decision of faith at a religious society meeting while listening to someone read an introduction to Romans written by Martin Luther. Wesley summed up his conversion with these now-famous words: "I felt my heart strangely warmed." Wesley not only heard about but experienced (*felt* and was drawn to) God's love that night.

Convinced that authentic faith springs from a *heartfelt response* to the love and grace of God—evidenced in the Bible and through the Spirit's continued work in the world—Wesley placed the heart at the center of Christian piety. As with Ignatius, he saw no contradiction—though certainly a good deal of tension—between this teaching and that which affirmed the importance of clear and reasonable thinking.

To resolve some of the tension, Wesley wrote zealously about the difference between affections and passions. Passions, he explained, are "involuntary emotions uninformed by either reason or the will—thus the danger of zeal without knowledge."[3] Affections, on the other hand, have been weighed sensibly and thoughtfully. They form the inner disposition of the heart.

Jonathan Edwards also insisted that emotions are central to spiritual life. In his 1746 work *A Treatise Concerning Religious Affections*, Edwards wrote, "There never was anything considerable brought to pass in the heart or life of any living man, by the things of religion, that had not his heart deeply affected by those things. . . . Upon the whole, I think it clearly and abundantly evident, that true religion lies very much in the affections."[4] Edwards believed that genuine emotional experience always comes with an understanding of and response to Truth. In no way, he explained, does this bypass the mind. Instead, our emotions work in concert with knowledge and choice.

Much of our education—Christian and academic—has taught us the opposite. We've been instructed to discount emotions and engage with pure and simple facts (as if such a thing exists). Western scholarship pretends that people can be strictly cerebral and completely impartial as they study information. Using words like *objective* and *detached,* some attempt to convince us that messy and complex emotions should be set aside, lest they undermine "real" learning.

In his book *Choices,* theologian Lewis Smedes issued a startling warning about this trend: "If we do not feel strongly about bad things, we may be neutralized, lukewarm, indifferent. And indifferent people do not care enough to make responsible choices. Many of us lived out years of our lives without a single strong feeling about racial discrimination . . . [but] some things have to be felt in order to be understood."[5]

Indeed.

Our feelings and thoughts are inextricably woven together. I agree with Christian philosopher Blaise Pascal, who goes so far as to claim that emotions are the *direct result* of thoughts.

Let's camp for a few moments on this essential matter, for as we more clearly discern the relationship between thoughts and feelings, we become more attuned to our whole hearts—will, understanding, and affections—and better prepared to make wise choices.

Passions . . . Affections . . . What Are You Feeling?

When they speak of emotions, particularly intense ones, people frequently use the words *passion* or *passionate.* Because these words imply a kind of passivity, many believe strong feelings "just happen" to them. But this simply isn't true. Each of us plays a continuous, active role in inviting and allowing our emotions to develop. We do so in the hidden realm of our thoughts.

In *Renovation of the Heart,* Dallas Willard explained this brilliantly: "There is no feeling without something being before the mind in thought and no thought without some positive or negative feeling toward what is contemplated."[6] For me, Willard's words help cement the assertions made by Ignatius, Wesley, and Edwards. If thoughts and feelings are completely interdependent, this explains why I cannot think about God without wanting to worship or wishing I could run away (depending on the state of my soul at any given moment).

How I think can determine how I feel in a number of ways as well. On a turbulent airplane, if I focus on the thought, *We're going to crash*, my anxiety level is sure to skyrocket. If I indulge insecure thoughts, my feelings toward other people will be suspicious and apprehensive. On a positive note, if I choose loving and kind thoughts, feelings of mercy and compassion flow from me.

The fear I may feel on a bumpy plane ride can be called a *primary emotion*. Immediate sensory input triggers thoughts, which then produce a feeling. This happens in a split-second process that we rarely stop to identify. And just because I experience a primary emotion—i.e. feeling anxious on a turbulent plane—does not mean that I distrust God. After taking in the sensory input and reviewing it, I can choose not to exacerbate that emotion with fearful thoughts. Instead, believing on the deepest level that God has my best in mind, I can bring a verse like this to mind: "My body and my mind may become weak, but God is my strength. He is mine forever" (Psalm 73:26, NCV).

Say, however, I live out of a deep-rooted fear that if people found out who I really am, they wouldn't love me. This belief would create *secondary emotions*—insecurity, doubt, anxiety—that then powerfully influence my choices. Secondary emotions arise after prolonged exposure to certain thoughts. Still very much feelings, these emotions reflect deep and underlying beliefs in a way that primary emotions do not.

Only repeatedly choosing to dwell on Truth can combat secondary emotions. For instance, a confident assurance of the truth found in Psalm 103:8-10 can produce the secondary emotion of peace even when insecurity threatens us. It says,

> The LORD is merciful and gracious;
>> he is slow to get angry and full of unfailing love.

> He will not constantly accuse us,
> > nor remain angry forever.
> He has not punished us for all our sins,
> > nor does he deal with us as we deserve. (NLT)

Here's the key point: In order to live well, we must courageously journey—with God—to the root of our issues, to the *reason* we're feeling certain emotions.

As feelings combine and build on one another, they eventually form moods and ultimately establish a person's emotional state. All of this affects an individual's ability to choose well. For example, people who live with the underlying belief (and its accompanying feelings) that they aren't "good enough" struggle. They may be hesitant to express their opinions, insecure in their body posture, and, because of their self-focus, generally unconnected with people around them. On the other hand, people who live in deep-seated faith (with its complementary affections) will—more with each day of maturity—present themselves confidently, overflow with compassion for others, and rest assured in their belovedness. Over time, the ongoing experience of particular feelings and repetitive indulgence of specific thoughts determine whether someone lives well or in resigned defeat.

In the sixteenth century, Saint Ignatius of Loyola recognized this powerful truth. Exploring the way emotions transform both the temporary and long-term course of our lives, Ignatius developed some incredibly helpful and practical ideas regarding discernment. Let's take a moment to look at his illuminating *Spiritual Exercises*.

Finding the Still Point

Ignatius of Loyola spent a good deal of his life in the Spanish military, learning and practicing the art of war. In his latter days, inspired by a dramatic call to commit his life to God's service, Ignatius invested energy training himself and others in a different art: the art of discernment.

In his book discussing the wisdom of Ignatius, Jesuit scholar Gerald O'Mahoney made this bold assertion:

> *Many of us have been taught to ignore our moods and to bash [continue] on regardless. No Christian teacher or preacher is likely to say "Ignore the Holy Spirit," yet, as [Ignatian wisdom] clearly shows, to ignore our moods is to ignore the Holy Spirit at work within us and amongst us. Noticing our moods, and learning to read them, is the first and indispensable step in discovering God's will for us.*[7]

Had we not already spent a good deal of time discussing how emotions affect our lives, this might seem like an extremely radical claim. But because we know that what we think and feel dramatically influences how we live, it makes absolute sense that the Holy Spirit would pull us toward feelings, thoughts, and ultimately mind-sets (moods) that would compel us to lovingly honor God, to want to do His will.

As Paul urged us in Philippians 4:6-8,

> *Don't fret or worry. Instead of worrying, pray. Let petitions and praises shape your worries into prayers, letting God know your concerns. Before you know it*, a sense of God's wholeness, *everything coming together for good*, will come and settle you down. *It's wonderful what happens when Christ displaces worry at the center of your life.*
>
> *Summing it all up, friends, I'd say you'll do best by filling your minds and meditating on things true, noble, reputable, authentic, compelling, gracious — the best, not the worst; the beautiful, not the ugly; things to praise, not things to curse.* (emphasis added)

When we fix our thoughts on what is true and good and right, rather than on what is worrisome, angering, or despairing, a "sense of God's wholeness" (a reasonable and confident *feeling* of God's peace)—far more wonderful than the human mind can understand—will keep our "hearts quiet and at rest" (Philippians 4:7, TLB).

What we think and feel leads us toward either serene confidence in God's good power or self-absorbed concern for our own well-being. We make wise and God-honoring decisions best at the "still point" Philippians 4 describes, the point at which our minds and hearts rest in God's transcendent peace. Ignatius called this "consolation."

We tend to equate the word *consolation* with comforting the sad or grieving. We console someone who has lost her spouse to death or his job to corporate downsizing. But in the Ignatian sense, consolation extends far beyond this singular meaning. Consolation encompasses all feelings that lead us toward wholeness and devotion, toward courage and strength, basically toward the things of God. In consolation, the Holy Spirit releases new energy, broadens our vision, and empowers us to do His will.

As Jesus proclaimed, "If you are thirsty, come to me! If you believe in me, come and drink! For the Scriptures declare that rivers of living water will flow out from within. (When he said 'living water,' he was speaking of the Spirit, who would be given to everyone believing in him" (John 7:37-39, NLT). The rivers of living water fuel the healing, hopeful, and faithful thought-feelings of consolation. Cultivating these emotions ultimately fosters moods of joy and peace. It also inspires others to live well.

The prophet Isaiah foretold a day when

> *leaders will make fair decisions.*
> *Then each ruler will be like a shelter from the wind,*
> *like a safe place in a storm,*
> *like streams of water in a dry land,*
> *like a cool shadow from a large rock in a hot land.*
> (Isaiah 32:1-2, NCV)

When we, God's holy nation of priests, make sound decisions, we experience—as well as provide for others—the security, nourishment, and covering of consolation.

It's essential to note, however, that consolation doesn't eliminate the pain of grief, injustice, rejection, or failure. Instead, it triumphs over agony by *walking through* it. Consolation hopes, rejoices, and courageously perseveres, whether the road is marked with suffering or sweetness.

Because of my natural bent toward passionate extremism, it would be easy for me to equate consolation with the spiritually high feelings I sometimes experience in my time with the Lord, at church, or when surrounded by His glory in nature (this is what my friend with the shower experience did). But, according to Ignatius, this is *not* consolation. Such raptures may lead to consolation, but they aren't the still point of peace at which decisions are best made.

After her shower experience, my friend felt "high"—empowered, inspired, and fervently committed to the "vision" she'd seen. But this would be what Scripture calls "zeal without knowledge" (Proverbs 19:2, NLT). Wisdom, on the other hand, recognizes that

enthusiasm without knowledge is not good.
     If you act too quickly, you might make a mistake.
(Proverbs 19:2, NCV)

Ignatius counseled followers of Jesus to remember that "even Satan can disguise himself as an angel of light" (2 Corinthians 11:14, NLT). I don't know what role Satan played in my friend's shower experience, but I do know that her subsequent emotional avoidance kept her for a time from becoming the woman God created her to be. Between the extremes of over-emotionalism and "cold reasoning" is the still point of consolation.

Recognizing that many Christians also swing from despondency ("I'll never be able to please God") to overexcitement ("I'm going to conquer the world for You, Lord!"), Ignatius encouraged people to listen carefully to the language of their moods, valuing stillness before God above fervor.

Consider the words of David, who confessed,

When things were going great
    I crowed, "I've got it made.
I'm GOD's favorite.
        He made me king of the mountain."
Then you looked the other way
        and I fell to pieces. (Psalm 30:6-7)

In his moment of strength, David believed he would never be shaken. He was "high" on the blessings and favor of the Lord. But when God's grace seemed far away, his zeal dissolved into bitter desolation.

As Ignatius informed us in *The Spiritual Exercises*, "It is character-istic of the evil spirit to cause gnawing anxiety, to sadden, and to set up obstacles. In this way the enemy unsettles . . . persons by false reasons, aimed at preventing their progress."[8] Remember, the Enemy wants to steal, kill, and destroy. He will discourage, stir up fear and sadness, make perseverance seem pointless, and always seek to topple those on a spiritual high.

Most Christians have experienced what we in youth ministry call "coming down the mountain." You go to a great conference or have an amazing time of worship and feel that "nothing can stop me now!" (Psalm 30:6, NLT). You're ready to make radical decisions or promis-es—to read your Bible for an hour every day, go on a mission to Iraq, or stay single forever (okay, maybe not that).

Then you "come down the mountain," and things fall apart.

Whether or not this happens after a spiritual "high," you experience what Ignatius called desolation. You're drained of energy and attracted to the gospel of self-gratification. God seems absent, His love a myth, and obeying Him burdensome.

In his book *The Call to Discernment in Troubled Times*, Dean Brackley commented on Ignatius's counsel: "The first rule when in desolation is, Don't make important changes! . . .When we are 'in the pits,' thoughts arise about changing our way of life. But when in turmoil . . . we lack the peace of mind needed to assess alternatives properly."[9] Such was the case after my friend discovered that Joel would not be her husband. Such is the wisdom my dad passed on with the words, "Don't make a decision at high tide."

When embroiled in intense emotions—whether positive *or* negative—we usually can't exercise sound judgment. We can, however, learn to discern our moods and the underlying beliefs driving them. When we find we are too high or too low, we can resist the urge to make decisions, asking God to bring us to the still point instead. This is how we can be at an emotional low tide when high-tide circumstances surround us.

At the still point, Ignatius wrote, "I am . . . in the middle and in equilibrium, ready in my mind to bring immediately all of myself to the side that I will recognize as conducing more to the divine glory and my salvation."[10] This he called "indifference."

Like the word *consolation*, *indifference* in today's usage differs from what Ignatius intended. Scholar George Gnass explained, "In no way does it mean unconcerned or unimportant." Instead, *indifference* implies "inner freedom from disordered inclinations."[11]

In the "Foundation," the paragraph around which the rest of his *Spiritual Exercises* revolves, Ignatius outlined the way to live well: Love only one thing (or rather some One). Ignatius's "Foundation" also details the most basic criteria for making wise decisions: Embrace One Love; reject all else.

This requires inner freedom (indifference). We must be free to choose, regularly and willingly, that which draws all lesser loves—like a magnet aligning iron filings—into the most powerful and only true Love. With indifference, we become less and less concerned with alternatives such as riches or poverty, honor or dishonor, a long life or a short one.

Dean Brackley commented,

> "Indifference" . . . is the capacity to sense and then embrace what is best, even when that goes against our inclinations. Indifference is neither stoic impassiveness nor the extinction of desire. . . . It means being so passionately and single-mindedly committed, so completely in love, that we are willing to sacrifice anything, including our lives, for the ultimate goal. It means magnanimous generosity, abandonment into God's hands, availability. It is not so much detachment from things as "detachability."[12]

This detachability, this inner freedom, allows us to find the still point. There, listening to the voice of the Holy Spirit becomes possible and habitual.

Usually, when faced with a big decision, we think the choice itself is difficult and making it well is our ultimate goal. But on closer inspection, we find the more challenging aspect is becoming free, allowing our lesser loves to be aligned by Love Himself. In this, the best choice becomes clear. But as you can imagine, this often takes time.

That's why when we *can* take time to consider our decisions, we absolutely should. Time allows us to evaluate our emotions, to let them calm down or come up, to sense the subconscious motivations and underlying beliefs that are compelling us to choose one alternative instead of another.

Of course, there will be moments when such pause and reflection are unrealistic or unattainable. We'll be asked to make split-second decisions. And both primary and secondary emotions will inevitably rush in. In cases such as these, having previously trained ourselves to listen for the Spirit's guidance through our emotions will be an indispensable aid. With practice, we can more readily incline ourselves to what God wishes us to do.

When faced with any choice, great or small, spontaneous or in the future, we can attune ourselves to the movements of desolation or consolation. We can even pretend that the decision is made and ask ourselves, *Does the prospect bring me feelings of darkness, hopelessness, or confusion? Does it bring me a sense of simplicity, lightness, and peace? Does it leave me numb, or does it send me into ecstasies?*

Questions such as these help us determine our emotional state, which then points back to what we are currently and regularly thinking or believing. It enables us to start making choices on the convictions and principles that we actually *want* to rule our lives, not on knee-jerk reactions.

In all of this, our goal is not to eliminate emotions that we "shouldn't feel." Again, if we look at the psalms, we'd be hard-pressed to claim that God sees any emotion as off-limits. Instead, we can use our emotions as a window to the depths of our hearts and, much more significantly, to the heart of God.

For instance, when we ask the hard questions that painful emotions prompt— "Does life make any sense?" "What is the purpose of suffering?" "Is God really good?" —we not only know His words to be true, but we experience their heart-transforming power.

Did you know that in Hebrew, the oft-quoted words of Psalm 46:10, "Be still, and know that I am God!" (NRSV), actually refer to an *experiential knowledge* that transcends simple intellectual acquaintance with a truth? These words speak of a deep and intimate spiritual-emotional connection with Truth.

Like a photographic negative, our dark feelings invert what

actually is. When developing a picture (the old-fashioned, nondigital way), everything black reflects what will become—through the refining process—light. Likewise, if we will press into our difficult emotions, God will transform even them, for "darkness is as light to [Him]" (Psalm 139:12, NRSV).

As Dan Allender and Tremper Longman beautifully expressed, "The irony of questioning God is that it honors Him: it turns our hearts away from ungodly despair toward a passionate desire to comprehend Him."[13] God doesn't merely want your robotic obedience. He wants the fervent engagement of your heart.

Your emotions—the good, the bad, and the ugly—allow you to *know* God, to *know* yourself. In this experiential knowledge, in staying close to the movements of consolation and desolation within your heart and mind, you can and will make decisions that honor God. You will neither overindulge your emotions nor downplay their significance.

Our feelings *do* matter. They *do* play a distinct, radically important role in our decision making. As we better learn to recognize their influence and appropriately respond, we become the kind of people whose lives are aligned completely by Love. And isn't this what we crave?

Questions for Discussion

1. Are you more tempted to give in to your emotions or to discount, ignore, and fear them? Why? What are some of the formative experiences or conversations you've had regarding the place of feelings in the Christian life? What did you learn from them? How do the words of this chapter strike you in comparison?

2. What do you think of the idea that ignoring our moods is equivalent to ignoring one of the primary ways the Holy Spirit works in our lives? If you agree with this, how would you explain it to

someone who has never heard such a thing? If you don't agree, what Scriptures or arguments support your position?

3. Can you think of a particular time when you experienced the Holy Spirit moving you toward an inner still point of quiet confidence in God? From what you remember of the experience, did your emotions match the description of consolation in this chapter? In what ways have you experienced desolation? Would you agree that being too high or too low makes wise decision making more challenging?

Thoughts for Personal Meditation

Is it difficult for you to believe that negative emotions can ultimately honor God? What do you make of Psalm 139:12, which says, "Darkness is as light to you" (NRSV)? What are some of the dark emotions you've felt (for example, grief, depression, or disappointment)? How might God refine them—like developing a photographic negative—into reflections of His light? How might looking for God's guidance, even in your dark emotions, help you make better decisions in the future?

A Prayer to Spark Your Conversation with God

Father, thank You for helping me discern the truth. My emotions and how they help me know what You're speaking to my heart are powerful gifts from You. I thank You for them. I also know that my heart is hopelessly dark and deceitful, a puzzle that no human can figure out. I need You to unravel the twisted feelings and thoughts of my innermost being. You, O God, search the heart and examine the mind. You know me and treat me as I really am, not as I pretend to be. You get to the bottom, to the very root of things. Help me understand what I feel and why. Let the fabric of my life be woven with Your thoughts and affections. Teach me to use my emotions for Your glory. Holy Spirit, I will listen to You. I will look to You for direction and wisdom. In the holy and all-powerful name of Jesus, amen.[14]

THREE

Sex, Beauty, and the Figure You Crave

DISCERNMENT AND YOUR BODY

A FEW MONTHS BEFORE my sixteenth birthday, I had the opportunity to travel around Europe for just shy of four weeks. My parents had been invited to minister through music at an outreach during the World's Fair that year in Seville, Spain. My sister Jessica and I joined their team as vocalists, but I don't think either of us looked forward as much to serving God as we did to seeing the Eiffel Tower and Venetian canals.

Little did I know that this trip would include two of the most radical spiritual experiences of my life, both wholly unconnected to the "official" ministry my family took part in.

The first occurred as I entered the museum in Italy that houses Michelangelo's *David*. We walked through the Academia doors at around 11 a.m., and it appeared the first rays of sun had just reached the skylights above David. There he stood, radiating sunlight, his muscular frame quietly contained in marble yet somehow pulsing with fierce strength.

A rush of adrenaline and an awestruck silence overtook me, immediately and absolutely separating me from the rest of the bustling crowd. As *David*'s beauty undid me, there was nothing I could do but worship. And though I didn't recognize it at the time, I had to choose in that moment *what* I would worship. It certainly would have been easy to praise the magnificent artistry and creative genius of Michelangelo. *David*'s undeniable glory could have compelled me to worship the statue itself. I could've celebrated the ideal beauty it conveyed. Or I could turn my attention to the Source of it all—the true Creator who continually inspires such splendor and skilled Michelangelo to express it.

Sad to say, those precious moments in the Academia faded rather quickly in the swirl of sights to see, great food to eat, and souvenirs to buy. But just one week later, I found myself overcome again by an exquisite majesty that I could neither explain nor hold on to.

For me, the main draw of St. Peter's Cathedral, located in the heart of Rome's Vatican City, was the famous Sistine Chapel. But it was actually when we exited the chapel and walked into the basilica beneath St. Peter's dome that I felt transported into another dimension. I wandered into what Celtic Christians first called a "thin space," a place where the veil between heaven and earth almost disappears.

Rays of brilliant morning sun shot through the stained glass around us and the ornately decorated windows above, leaving dazzling pools of sunlight (like those I'd recently observed illuminating *David*) on the cathedral's marbled floor. I lifted my head to heaven and stepped into one luminous shaft, feeling its warmth and power. From across the capella, my mom took several pictures of me standing in what the camera captured as the natural beauty of rising sun and splendid architecture.

But what film and print could never convey was the irrepressible urge to worship that mounted in me, standing in a space that became progressively "thinner." If the hundreds of other visitors to St. Peter's had instantly vanished, I'm sure I would have shouted something like, "Hallelujah!"

All this I sensed organically and overwhelmingly, even though I wasn't particularly close to God at the time. I knew a lot about Him and really thought I loved Him. But I had not yet tasted and seen His goodness.

In fact, though it's sad for me to admit, I initially didn't want to go to Europe "just to serve God." I could barely stand the thought of missing nearly four weeks of summer activities with friends. And I was afraid—though not as much as I would be on subsequent vacations—about what I would eat and when I would exercise during our trip.

A conflicted relationship between me and my body, which I could neither ignore nor control, had only recently begun to escalate. Over the years that followed, my body distress swelled to a nearly consuming ferocity. But on that trip, I didn't genuinely *fear*, as I later would, things like chocolate croissants or butter on my vegetables.

This, however, is not the time or place to detail such matters. I have done so elsewhere.[1] Here, it's most relevant to note that after my trip to Europe, a protracted struggle with body image and eating issues prevented me from processing experiences like the ones I had at St. Peter's and the Academia.

Indeed, five years of largely wasted (as in, devoted to the wrong causes) mental and physical energy would fly by before I could recognize the significance of my time abroad. But as I graduated from college and began to embrace my body and the beauty God called me to express with it, I understood with rich clarity what I only sensed at fifteen.

When Paul declared "each of us a temple in whom God lives" (2 Corinthians 6:16), I think the apostle confuses (sometimes angers) a lot of women. One reason is obvious: Few of us really like our bodies, so positive statements about them often feel false or hopelessly idealistic. But years later, remembering those evocative experiences of my European adventure, I discovered that Paul's statement also confused and frustrated me because I simply couldn't relate to the term *temple*.

Before that trip, I equated *temple* with the religious meeting places I worshipped in. They were holy places, but only in the sense that the buildings were "set apart" for the purpose of spiritual things. Though there may have been some attempt at creating a comfortable and pleasant environment, *beauty* clearly was not the central goal of the evangelical architecture with which I was familiar. The churches I had been in were primarily functional in nature. I had never experienced church or my body as a "temple," let alone a space of commanding beauty like the ones that overwhelmed me in Italy.

But staring at *David*'s powerful body gleaming in midmorning radiance and wandering into a shaft of the same luminous glow in St. Peter's Cathedral violently and eternally rearranged my understanding of Paul's comparison. In the Academia and St. Peter's, my body *felt* as if it could be a temple. I was surrounded by beauty, participating in beauty, worshipping not ethereal beauty but the Eternal Beauty I want to and *can* reflect.

When Paul likened our bodies to a temple, he did so not only to emphasize that we are "the home of the living God," but also to remind us that with our bodies we are continually invited to experience and express His splendor.

Exquisite majesty defined every single temple of antiquity, whether the pagan Parthenon or the glorious temple built in Solomon's day for

Yahweh, the True and Living God. Beauty was not merely an after-thought. Hebrews and heathens alike believed in an eternal connection between loveliness of form (physically and architecturally) and the Divine.

As N. T. Wright observed in *Simply Christian*, the ancient Israelites' belief in the overlap of heaven and earth focused intently on the temple in Jerusalem. For the Hebrews, the temple was more than a place. It was where heaven and earth interlocked.[2]

Contemporary Christians have lost or discarded most of this thinking. Recently, some attempts at recapturing a vision of beauty as essential and God-honoring have been made. But on the whole, evangelical Christians are still incredibly uncomfortable with beauty.

When the physical body is discussed in church, it's usually done so with a warning tone and a proverbially wagging finger. Can you imagine someone preaching this Sunday that your body is a beautiful place where heaven and earth overlap and interlock? Instead (mostly), well-meaning pastors quote a verse like

> *Charm can fool you, and beauty can trick you,*
> > *but a woman who respects the LORD should be praised.*
> *(Proverbs 31:30, NCV)*

and leave it at that.

For many women, this (and similarly misinterpreted verses such as 1 Peter 3:3-5) communicates a false message: Beauty doesn't matter to God and shouldn't matter to "good Christians." If you care about your body or want to be attractive, you're vain and disobedient. And that's not even getting into the cautions churchgoers receive about their sexuality.

What tragic misapplications of God's Word we're sometimes fed! While it's absolutely true that we must guard against vanity and rebellious focus on ourselves and while it is absolutely imperative that we squarely face the way our sexuality can mislead and master us, it is *just as* important that we remember that with discernment, each of us can experience our body as "a showplace of God's greatness" (1 Corinthians 6:19-20).[3]

Our bodies matter to God for positive reasons, not merely because of the prohibitions connected to them. Beauty matters to God. We sense this inherently but have been inundated for so long with the message that our bodies and beauty are neutral at best, hell-bent at worst.

The complicated way people misconstrue God's view of beauty influences how we see our bodies and how we use them. And the mess seems nowhere more extraordinarily evident than in female sexuality. Most women struggle with finding a positive body image, as well as with what they're supposed to think about and then do with sexual desires.

But God shows us that beauty and sexuality can be bridges. Through beauty, through your body, and through what you do with your body, you can experience God in ways you might never ask for or imagine.

The straightforwardness of Scripture leaves no doubt: *Your* body is a temple. The Bible doesn't say, "Your body is a temple, but only if it's a size X or if you maintain it with healthy eating and exercise." It doesn't proclaim, "Your body is primarily functional. Though you will feel powerful sexual urges, the most important thing you can do is control them." It never advises, "Don't try to understand your sexuality; nobody can."

No. The Word of God proclaims the goodness and glory of sexuality and of every body . . . of *your* body. Picture with me an awesome "thin space" like those I described earlier. This is how God sees your body—a masterpiece of His design.

Can you believe that? Do you want to believe that?

If you do, let's look at how discernment can help us recapture three important aspects of enjoying the body God's given you.

You're Beautiful, It's True

In a particularly challenging section of *Renovation of the Heart*, Dallas Willard observed that for better or for worse, your body lies at the very center of a God-honoring life. This statement often surprises or confuses Christians, Willard noted, despite the fact that even the most basic understanding of human nature reveals that for most people, the body is a primary obstacle in the process of sanctification.[4]

Applying the idea Willard introduced here, I'd posit that for most women, body image (and the way women feel about themselves as a result of their body image) forms a major roadblock to joy and peace in their relationship with God.

Thankfully, once we recognize the central role our bodies and the thoughts we have about them play in the greater drama of our lives, the words of Paul about our physicality and sexuality make much more sense. Without acknowledging this, however, the words of Scripture become dangerously disconnected from our daily lives.

Most Christians could tell you that God created humans in His image. What they may not be able to articulate, however, is how this applies to their own specific body. In *Practical Mysticism*, scholar Evelyn Underhill explained that being created in His image makes each person "a living, ardent tool with which the Supreme Artist works: one of the instruments of His self-manifestation, the perpetual process by which His Reality is brought into concrete expression."[5] Underhill then urged us to consider a penetrating question: "Do you proclaim by your existence the grandeur, the beauty, the intensity, the living wonder of that Eternal Reality within which, at this moment, you stand?"[6]

Here's what I wanted to ask after first reading this query: "Is that even *possible*?"

If we are created to "image" (to reflect, picture, and represent) God—who in no uncertain terms defines Himself as grand, beautiful, intense, and eternally wonderful—not only can we believe that it's possible to do so, but we can also *fully expect* to proclaim these divine attributes by our existence and through our very bodies.

The trouble is that though we long to reveal grandeur and beauty, we usually go about it in a disastrously upside-down way. Twenty years ago, Allan Bloom, author of *The Closing of the American Mind*, noted that college students "have powerful images of what a perfect body is and pursue it incessantly. But deprived of . . . guidance, they no longer have any image of a perfect soul, and hence do not long to have one. They do not even imagine that there is such a thing."[7] Most college graduates are no better off.

Somehow, we've come to believe that having a "perfect body" will make us more attractive to people and better able to handle life. Christians, along with the world as a whole, have bought into the lie that being fit or toned (or whatever word we might use) will give us more time, energy, and power to do and get what we want. In the daily business and busyness of life, we live—without much thought—in the lies that we are what we look like, we'd be happier if we looked like _____, and we'd be better Christians if we got a handle on our body issues.

And though we're bombarded by messages about our bodies from every angle, though body-image battles constantly confront us, though more and more Christians find themselves in the grips of eating disorders (whether characterized by overeating, undernourishing, or purging), churches rarely acknowledge the importance of developing a right body image. Perhaps eating disorders or body image are discussed in youth groups or at special seminars, but that's about it.

In their excellent book *Why Beauty Matters*, Cynthia Hicks and Karen Lee-Thorp observed,

> *Neither of us has ever heard a sermon about body image in a Sunday morning service, even though we're willing to bet that nearly every man in the congregation has evaluated some woman's attractiveness (or lack thereof) . . . during the service, and nearly every woman has evaluated her own looks — and possibly those of the women around her — during the same time period.*[8]

How much time have I wasted (some during Sunday service and some even after I became a pastor's wife) taking note of where I stack up against the women around me? How ashamed would I be if some cosmic clock had been keeping track and one day revealed just how many hours I've consumed evaluating myself over and against those who are supposed to be my sisters in Christ, my allies?

With these words, God used Paul to lead us to joyful conviction:

> *Since this is the kind of life we have chosen, the life of the Spirit, let us make sure that we do not just hold it as an idea in our heads or a sentiment in our hearts, but work out its implications in every detail of our lives. That means we will not compare ourselves with each other as if one of us were better and another worse. We have far more interesting things to do with our lives. Each of us is an original.* (Galatians 5:25-26)

Whether we recognize it or not, the life we crave is the "life of the Spirit" to which Paul referred. Many of us have chosen to pursue this life at some point. But we often allow it to dissolve into an empty "idea in our heads or a sentiment in our hearts."

God's admonition — to "work out its implications in every detail of our lives"—includes a call to view our bodies in the light of six incredibly important words:

Each of us is an original.

Original means that not all of us will wear a certain size or weigh the same amount. *Original* means that we can let go of the lie, "I would be happier if I just had a body like _____." *Original* means we have "*far more interesting things to do with our lives*" than "compare ourselves with each other as if one of us were better and another worse."

My question to the broken heart within me and to every person reading these words is this: Do we really believe that we have far more interesting things to do with our lives? If we inventoried, for instance, the amount of time women spend on looking good and making sure men—and sometimes even more important, other women—notice, we'd be hard-pressed to claim that we put stock in God's words.

When she published the best-selling book *The Beauty Myth: How Images of Beauty Are Used Against Women*, journalist Naomi Wolf revealed, "Urban professional women are devoting up to a third of their income to 'beauty maintenance,' and considering it a *necessary* investment."[9]

We might be shocked at this statistic—a third of their income!—until we add up what *we* spend on merchandise for our bodies: facial cleansers and moisturizers, lotions, bath gels, hairstyling implements and products (let alone haircuts, weaves, perms, or coloring), manicures, pedicures, makeup, perfume, gym memberships, and diet foods or aids. The list goes on and on. Now please don't misunderstand me. My goal in pointing this out is *not* to claim that any of these things are inherently bad, nor even to emphasize what many before me have said: out of balance, the pursuit of beauty can become idolatrous.

My desire in acknowledging these trends and getting each of us to think about where we fall on the continuum is to help us recognize that we often perpetuate the body-image comparison game. Even those who spend next to nothing on beauty products may unwittingly propagate the myth that there is a right way to treat the body. Naturalists may look down on those who enjoy makeup or other merchandise and think themselves better because they do not "need" or "waste their money on" such things.

In *Reviving Ophelia*, Dr. Mary Pipher rightly noted that teen-age girls are "the biggest enforcers and proselytizers for the culture [obsessed with the body]. . . . They punish by walking up to girls with insults about their clothes or bodies. They punish by nicknames and derogatory labels."[10]

Adult women rarely kick one another verbally. We kick under our breath instead. We kick at each other behind closed doors, gossiping with friends. We kick *ourselves* for not being like _____, who is so disciplined with what she eats and how often she exercises.

Do we not have more interesting things to do with our lives? Do we not have another choice?

This is where discernment and body image collide. We *do* have other options. We *can* choose to end the body-image contest, at least in our own lives. By our example, we can inspire others to do the same. And we need discernment to do it. So here are a couple of practical ways to start.

Make conscious choices to avert your eyes from the things that spark body envy and despair—and let me tell you, I personally need to do this many times a day!

A recent survey found that 70 percent of women felt ashamed, guilty, and discouraged after looking at a fashion magazine for only three minutes.[11] Do you know what I have to say to that? *Three* minutes? Ha! I sometimes feel shameful, guilty, and depressed after checking out at the grocery store. Even glancing at the covers of *People* and *Cosmo* can make me feel frumpy, "less than," and angry.

Until mass media and mass transportation became part of everyday life, most people lived in small towns and came into contact with no more than one hundred women *in their entire lives*. Today, we see not only hundreds of women in our own spheres but also approximately six hundred of the most beautiful women in the whole world (that's about how many female models and movie stars we see in a lifetime). And those six hundred are culled from thousands of aspiring celebrities.[12]

Not only are we repeatedly exposed to the crème de la crème of physical beauty but we're taught to measure ourselves against them. Now is the time to decide to stop, to discern when to *look away*. We don't have to peruse, let alone buy, fashion magazines or star-track rags. We don't have to watch movies that tempt us to compare ourselves with gorgeous celebs who spend hours a day in the gym and do crazy things like put *hemorrhoid cream* on puffy, unrested eyes or duct tape on sagging breasts.

Of course, there's no inherent evil in magazines or movies. And I have no idea how much these visual images affect you; that's a matter for you and God to sort out. What I do know is this: Determining to avert my eyes is a place to start, a place where discernment has helped — and continues to help — me find more interesting things to do with my time and body than compare and evaluate.

If you agree to try turning your gaze you may well wonder, *What do I look at instead?* Many of us have focused on our own bodies and those of others for so long that comparison has become habitual and consuming. We need discernment in averting our eyes and also in choosing where to place them.

Sadly, as Brennan Manning noted in *The Ragamuffin Gospel*, "Our world has lost its sense of wonder. . . . We no longer catch our breath at the sight of a rainbow or the scent of a rose, as we once did. We have grown bigger and everything else smaller, less impressive. We get blasé and worldly wise and sophisticated."[13] Many of us have become immune to the splendor around us. We no longer see the beauty permeating our world, let alone the beauty that is within each of us, original works of supreme artistry.

As we turn our eyes from the media images, from the scale, from the tape measure that the world uses to calibrate our worth, we can once again celebrate what Saint Augustine called the beauty around and in us: "a stairway to the immortal and enduring." And as we recapture a childlike wonder that appreciates the glory of creation, the cares of body image become smaller and less impressive.

Right or wrong, messages I heard at church in the past led me to believe that only inner beauty should matter to Christians. But this never satisfied the craving of my heart to experience and express splendor and glory in tangible ways. Worried and confused about my appearance, I felt discontented with the talks urging me to focus only on the "inner me." But what I didn't understand at the time was this: The fact that beauty radiates from within does not eradicate but ultimately *elevates* external expressions of beauty. It turns the physical beauty we see and experience back to the Creator and Sustainer of beauty.

Let's turn our attention now to exploring how discernment helps us participate — in right and good ways — in the dynamic relationship between inner radiance and external beauty.

Beautiful One, I Love; Beautiful One, I Adore

What words do you automatically associate with God? Holiness, righteousness, truth, goodness, love, mercy, grace? What about beauty — beauty manifested in physical and tangible ways?

When the junior high group at our church asked me to speak on the topic of beauty, I was amazed at the number of times throughout Scripture that God is described by Himself or by others as beautiful (see, for instance, Revelation 4:3; Psalm 50:2; and Psalm 27:4). Radiantly, magnificently, gloriously *beautiful* is our God.

And we are created in His image. *You* are created in His gorgeous image.

In her sinless state, Eve revealed God's image in a way that none of us will ever fully comprehend or recapture. Though we know nothing of her physical features, we do know that before the Fall, Eve perfectly reflected what God created her to be—a representative of Himself on earth. Because He is beautiful, God undoubtedly imaged His splendor in Eve.

Deep within, each of us senses that God intended us to reflect His beauty in the pure and lovely ways a sinless Eve once did. This explains why we both love and hate, are in awe of and envy the touched-up-to-perfection images of models and actresses: They hint at an untarnished beauty hidden within us.

Indeed, all beauty woos us to a world both beyond and within. Yet as author N. T. Wright keenly observed,

> *The world is full of beauty but the beauty is incomplete. Our puzzlement about what beauty is, what it means, and what (if anything) it is there for is the inevitable result of looking at one part of a larger whole. We climb the mountain, and though the view from the summit is indeed magnificent, it leaves us wanting more. . . . Indeed, the beauty sometimes seems to be in the itching itself, the sense of longing, the kind of pleasure which is exquisite and yet leaves us unsatisfied.*[14]

Far more than the dazzling view from a mountaintop, far more than the sparkling glory of the stars above, we—created to bear God's image in a way that nature never can—can point people to the only Beauty who won't leave us hungry for more. We can show others that it's the larger whole they long for, not merely the "part" (the toned body, the flawless complexion, the perfectly put-together ensemble). As we radiate beauty from the inside out, the "itching" for heaven becomes more real than ever.

So how do we *do* this?

One way we can practically work out these truths is by acknowledging the manifestations of beauty in those around us. As we purposefully and consistently recognize the unique expression of God's beauty in one another, we participate in the glorious project God began by imaging Himself in humans.

William Gurnall once commented, "It is this image of God reflected in you that so enrages hell; it is this at which the demons hurl their mightiest weapons."[15] Beauty is a battleground on which countless victims have fallen prey to the slings and arrows of our Enemy. As we affirm the beauty that God places within others, we war against the lies of hell that strip individuals of their dignity and worth.

And when we look on others with a love that confirms and confers beauty, we bring healing to the walking wounded. Authors Cynthia Hicks and Karen Lee-Thorp rightly noted that people "don't need to *be* beautiful, but they do need to be loved in ways that make them *feel* beautiful."[16] Love calls out of each of us the beauty that is within, the beauty that has been scarred and buried and/or traded for the pseudo-glory offered by the world.

We've all observed how those we love become more beautiful before our eyes. Love can transform anyone, even a person the world cruelly judges as plain or dumpy. Love reveals splendor in any human for God's glory.

Because beauty radiates from the inside out, the inner harmony that being loved and noticed produces inevitably creates glory that can be seen and touched, beauty that points others back to the Source. All of us feel the need to be seen, to be appreciated, to be noticed. But tragically, we often withhold our love and encouragement from others. Maybe we're afraid that in acknowledging the beautiful image of God in them, we'll take something away from ourselves. But believe me, there's more than enough of God's beauty to go around.

My own challenge, and a challenge I'd issue to everyone, is to call out the beauty in those around us. Decide with me to look for and help reveal the splendor of God by noticing and appreciating the original glory of every person in our lives. As we do so, the beauty we've chosen to see in others will shine through us as well. In this way, the life of beauty we crave rightly and unself-consciously becomes ours.

And Finally, the Good News About Sex

A final and extraordinarily important aspect of discernment and the body is how we use the beautiful, original works of art God created us to be. Though we cannot unpack the mystery completely, let's look for a few moments at how we apply discernment to our sexuality.

In his candid book *Sex for Christians*, Lewis Smedes wisely identified that "the toughest problem Christians have with sex is how to feel about their own sexuality. On this subject many of us are confused, confounded, and inconsistent. . . . Some Christians feel that their sexuality is nature's strongest competitor for their loyalty to Christ: their feelings tell them that sexuality is not a sweet gift of creation but a bitter fruit of the fall."[17]

Christians also tend to view sex solely in terms of negative rules: Don't do it until you're married, don't do it with anyone but your spouse, don't masturbate, don't look at porn . . . don't, don't, don't. These are important prohibitions, but we cannot get so caught up in the don'ts that we miss the *positive force* behind God's standards. The beauty of marital fidelity forms the law against adultery. And behind the vigorous arguments against impurity lies God's incredibly affirming view of sex and human sexuality.

Yet because of the Fall, Christians must forever discern between God's gifts in creation and sin's distortions of them. As we talk about and live out the sexual freedom God intended to give us, discernment becomes incredibly significant.

Some people define sexual freedom as the ability to have sex whenever and with whomever one pleases. But freedom always involves two dimensions: what we are free *for* and what we are free *from*.

Sexual freedom in a loose, worldly way may be freedom *for* something, but it brings bondage to other things. It shrinks sexuality into an endless search for personal pleasure and perfect technique. It makes sex about orgasm and opportunity. It enslaves those who seek freedom to an idolatry that promises everything and delivers little more than the physical experience of fingers playing with our body, the mental experience of porn-inspired fantasy, or the penetration of a fleeting moment of pleasure.

To make an idol, all people need to do is selectively parcel up reality, separating what they worship from the whole of creation. We make an idol of sex when we expect too much good from it or fear too much evil from it.

Only God-given sexual freedom, freedom *for* the best sex possible and *from* the complications that undiscerning sexuality brings (which leads to either loose morals or unhealthy fear), can truly liberate us.

In light of this, Smedes remarked,

> *Marriage is not just a God-given lid to clamp down on an impulse that, left free to roam, could reduce life to chaos, or, suppressed, could leave a person "aflame with passion" (1 Corinthians 7:9). In marriage, the radical self-giving, the unique self-exposure, and the unreserved sharing of selves that sex really aims at is given its best chance for success. Marriage is not just for the control of sex: It is for the liberation and fulfillment of sex.*[18]

Unfortunately, most of what people know about sex is of a shallow, skin-on-skin variety. But God's view of sex and sexuality is incredibly positive and incredibly complex. As 1 Corinthians 6:16 clearly reveals, "There's more to sex than mere skin on skin. Sex is as much spiritual mystery as physical fact. As written in Scripture, 'The two become one.'"

Though our sexual desires move us toward intimate relationship and companionship, though our sexual drives remind us—sometimes painfully so—that we long to be fully known and to know another completely as well, we still sometimes trade the mysterious beauty of sexual acts for the physical passion we see played out in the movies.

Many people, even many Christians, see sexual expressions (from kissing to intercourse) as a special form of intimacy, but not necessarily as life-uniting acts. Though the apostle Paul clearly equated intercourse with a total life union, his "one flesh" rhetoric rarely communicates to the average person, churchgoing or not.

Today, the most powerful descriptor of sexual expression is the media, not the Bible. As *Sex for Christians* notes, "Its seductive lure is almost overwhelming. It is difficult to imagine that any young person who watches today's films [or television] regularly could ever again feel—let alone think—about sexual intercourse in the same way that his parents did."[19] And the sex we see on TV and the silver screen, the sex we read about in *Glamour* or romance novels, the sex that is daily splashed on billboards and talked about at coffee shops around the country just isn't very mysterious.

Discernment, the right ordering of our thinking and feeling, helps us reestablish the glorious and transcendent mystery of God's gifts in sexuality and sex. One way we can work toward this is by purposefully avoiding the kind of easy familiarity that we have with other people's bodies, whether in conversation or action.

As a teenager, I regularly talked about and dwelt on the sculpted bodies of male actors or models. This did nothing to connect me with the mystery of sex, which is what I *actually* craved. Giving "innocent" back rubs or playful tickles didn't make me better able to deal with my sexual drives. Watching sex scenes—though women are supposedly less visual than men (a point I would argue in light of the fact that more and more women are now ensnared by Internet pornography)—did *not* give me better information about sex but rather a comfortableness with the act of sex that belied what God intended it to be—a sacrament, a "visible sign of an invisible grace."[20]

For many, instead of a sacrament, sex and sexuality become toys.[21] Toys that relieve the pressures of daily life. Toys that promise escape from the boredom and bothers, anxiety and anger, loneliness and lovelessness that often threaten us. Whether through fantasy or masturbation, sexual expression before or outside of marriage, we sometimes use sex—in thought or deed—as a diversion from reality.

Instead, we can use discernment as a tool that redeems and reestablishes us in reality, even its most painful moments. Carefully discerning what experience has taught us and what we observe in others allows us to recognize these truths:

- Indulging sexual desire doesn't permanently relieve tension but only temporarily fills the vacuum inside, a vacuum that even the inevitably increasing tempo of physical touch can never completely fill.
- Fantasy—even the seemingly innocuous forms inspired by some romantic shows, films, or novels—leaves us unfulfilled, unsatisfied, and longing for an illusion, for something that could never exist in reality.
- Repeated exposure to pornography makes sex trivial, unexciting, and lifeless. More than any other compulsion, it empties sex of mystery, wonder, and hunger for union.

- Obsessive masturbation disconnects sex from the personal, life-uniting dimension of our sexuality.

Discernment also helps us separate attraction from lust. I recall mentoring Taylore, a young single woman eager to commit her whole life to the Lord. She once hesitatingly and apologetically admitted that she was interested in a young man partly because he was cute. Taylore quickly emphasized this wasn't the only reason she found Mark attractive, but I stopped her midsentence: "Taylore, it's okay to notice when people are good-looking. It's not automatically lust, you know."

She seemed incredibly relieved and also a bit curious. I don't think anyone had helped Taylore discern between attraction and lust. And though some of you may be better equipped than Taylore was to make that distinction, there are *many* Christians who experience immediate guilt when drawn to a good-looking person. But we simply cannot equate every erotic feeling with lust. How cruel would it be if God created so many attractive people but forbade us to even notice them?

Discernment helps us recognize when we're simply aware of someone's attractiveness and when we're dominated by sexual desire. Synthesizing some modern and ancient thoughts on the subject of Christian sexuality, I've developed a couple of distinctions between lust and attraction:

- Noticing people and feeling attracted to them is a natural part of human life. Our minds and bodies respond to pleasurable sights, sounds, smells, and experiences. Being drawn to a particular someone starts in the mind, as we process the physical impulses that signal, "Hey! Check him out." Like any other instinctive thought, however, we can become captivated by the combination of idea and image that makes up attraction. When we allow sexual thoughts to ensnare us (to make us their captives), we begin to lust.

- Because attraction is natural and intuitive, people usually can't determine who they will be drawn to. Lusting after someone, on the other hand, includes a *decision* to dwell on the arousal we feel around a particularly attractive person. Lust pushes noticing someone's charms from the level of awareness to *intention*. Fanning the flame of desire to "what I would do" or even "what I would like to do but know I shouldn't" leads to lust.

Both married and single Christians need this kind of sexual discernment. If you think that being attracted to members of the opposite sex stops once you put on a wedding ring, I'm sorry to break it to you: It doesn't! Making wise decisions about dealing with your sexuality is a lifelong business.

I like the way one godly married man I know deals with noticing beautiful women. If an attractive woman catches his eye, he directs his thoughts to God in this way: "Thank You, Lord, for that beautiful flower." He actually articulates this if he's with a group of guys who all notice the same girl. Instead of indulging in the "Did you see her?" conversation, he gives glory to God for His creative genius.

We praise God for the majesty of the Rocky Mountains, for the sweet beauty of a sleeping baby, for the mighty roar of the ocean as it breaks on the shore. Why not thank Him for attractive people? As we turn our minds to God, little room will be left for lust and its ofttimes companion, fantasy.

A Story Still Unfolding

We write the story of our lives with each decision we make. And a large portion of our story deals with how we respond to and express our sexuality. So an essential question to ask—and to continue asking throughout our lives—is this: Am I composing my own story, which includes sexuality, in a manner that fits with and reflects the greater story God is telling through humanity?

It would do each of us good to ponder this question, not only in regard to sexuality, but when considering everything we think about or do with our bodies: Are we writing stories with our body image and beauty that harmonize with God's story?

At different stages of our lives, we may answer with a grateful "Yes! You have helped me to honor You, Lord." Other times we'll be moved to repentance and grief as we recognize the story we've been writing opposes God's.

No matter where you are presently, where you've come from, or where you might go in the future, God's ongoing story of redemption will always have room for you. As you continue or turn back to writing your life story with Jesus, you will experience greater freedom with your body.

I urge you, brothers and sisters, in view of God's mercy, to present your bodies as living sacrifices. Your body—yes, *your* body—is holy and acceptable to Him, a great work of His artistry. Do not conform to the ideas of this world that you must look like X to be loved or that your sexuality means Y. Be transformed, by the renewing of your mind, so that you might discern the will of God for your life and for your body—the good, pleasing, and perfect will that restores your rightful and beautiful inheritance, His image in you.

Questions for Discussion

1. What would it look like if Christians became allies—rather than competitors or enemies—in battling the myth that beauty equals being the "right" size, shape, color, or degree of put-togetherness? Discuss or journal about the practical suggestions this chapter made.

2. How might we use what we've learned to help men around us understand the tension women feel between the unhealthy

pressure to be beautiful according to impossible worldly standards, and the glorious truth that we were created to reveal Beauty? Which men in your life might you discuss these ideas with in order to spread the word about discernment and the body?

3. In his book *Christian Modesty and the Public Undressing of America*, Jeff Pollard wrote, "Excess and sensuality—both of these bear on modesty. . . . If they are modest, [people] will not draw attention to themselves in the wrong way. Their dress will not say 'SEX!' or 'PRIDE!' or 'MONEY!,' but 'purity,' 'humility' and 'moderation.'"[22] What does your own way of dressing say? Sex? Pride? Money? Insecurity? I don't care? Beauty doesn't matter? How might your dress reflect or detract from God's image in you?

Thoughts for Personal Meditation

Find some pictures of a beautiful church, perhaps one you've visited or would like to visit someday. Allow God to show you how your body, much more so than this earthly temple, is a glorious home for Him and a reflection of His splendor. As your heart resists or assents, talk to God about your feelings. Ask Him to reveal His image in you in a way you've never noticed before.

A Prayer to Spark Your Conversation with God

Lord, my body is an extension of my deepest self. I desire to present to You and those around me a body that directs others to worship You. I acknowledge my hunger for beauty and offer You thanks for the spark of glory You put in me at creation. Forgive me for failing to recognize Your splendor in me. Help me to reorder my thoughts and to discern what is right and good about my body and my sexuality. Today, by Your power within me, Holy Spirit, I intend to worship You with my body.

FOUR

Stopping the Flow

HOW DISCERNMENT TRANSFORMS WHAT YOU SAY

THERE ARE FEW PEOPLE I enjoy conversing with as much as Tanya. While expressing the ideas she's reading about, wrestling with, and trying to assimilate into her life, Tanya continually inspires me. Love and longing for God permeate her words.

But Tanya freely admits that this wasn't always the norm for her. Because God has taught her a great deal about discernment in using and receiving words, I asked Tanya to share some of her story with us. I know her thoughts will encourage and challenge you, as they do me.

Sarcasm 101

I grew up in a large family, the youngest of six children. We always gathered together for the evening meal, and I have vivid memories of our raucous dinnertimes.

Our family table overflowed with good food, many words,

and much laughter. The laughter, however, often came at someone's expense—someone less capable of defending herself against the onslaught of belittling words and sarcasm. This was usually my sister Joyce.

I remember feeling angry and helpless because no one came to Joyce's aid. I would sit in my chair, hoping and praying that she would not react, not give them the satisfaction. But over and over again, Joyce took their bait.

My brothers were like playground bullies who went unchallenged and undisciplined. If any complaint was made, they mercilessly chastised their victim (whether Joyce or someone else): "Can't you take a joke? Lighten up! What's your problem?"

Watching this, I learned that words can be powerful—both as weapons and as shields. But not only did I observe the power of words at our family table, I also began to sharpen my skills in wielding them. In this, I made a life-changing discovery.

Growing up in an environment of neglect and abuse, I spent much of my childhood feeling afraid. I found that the skillful use of words made me formidable, a less desirable mark. So I became quick on my feet and sharp-tongued, able to take someone apart verbally with razorlike precision. I used my "talent" to protect myself and defend others who were being victimized.

As I grew into a very direct and forthright person, I developed little tolerance or patience for those who played games with words or communicated indirectly. They suffered from the slings and arrows of my intentionally aimed scorn.

Over time, my verbal responses became so automatic that I no longer possessed them, but rather they possessed me. I began to see that the very words I believed had saved me in childhood and young adulthood, the same ones that had kept me from dangerous vulnerability, now kept me at a distance from people I cared about. True intimacy would be impossible for me as long as my (mostly) bitter tongue continued to direct the course of my relationships.

I received Jesus Christ as my Lord and Savior at the age of thirty-two. He filled my heart with a deep love and longing for Him — a desire to know Him and be known by Him. He also made it absolutely clear that my words needed changing.

More important, He revealed that my heart, which caused me to speak with venom and sarcasm, needed to be transformed. After my conversion, even if the hurtful things I wanted to say (or, much to my sorrow and regret, would say) were true, I knew that it was out of the overflow of a wounded and wicked heart that my mouth spoke.

Jesus also showed me that words hold the power of life (see Ephesians 4:29) and death (see James 3:5-6). The choices I make about what to say (and, just as important, what not to say) dramatically affect other people.

Empowered by the Holy Spirit, I've decided — over and over again — to drop my own defenses, seek transparency, and give up my "right" to speak in certain ways. Some time ago, I made a personal commitment to encourage people whenever possible. I believe this choice further propelled the process of my inner transformation — of Christ being fully formed in me.

But I won't pretend it's always been easy to seek my neighbor's good, speaking words that build up and edify instead of those that humorously tear down. At first, I found trying to carry through with my decision incredibly difficult and disheartening. I didn't recognize that I was attempting to change myself, to control my tongue through my own strength. Each time I failed, I became very discouraged. No matter how deeply I desired it, I couldn't force an internal transformation through external actions. I now know that actions can reveal my obedience or disobedience, but they cannot change my heart.

Inner transformation is the work of the Holy Spirit. By

surrendering myself to God and asking Him to make His thoughts my thoughts, His heart for others my heart, and His words my words, I find that more and more His will becomes my own.

Still, the most difficult aspect of using and receiving words in a God-honoring way continues to be this submitting to God, this dying to my "old self." Though my will is to speak words of life, there are times I struggle fiercely with the habit, rooted deep within my flesh, to speak words of death.

Whether they sound humorous or hateful, I don't want to speak words that add to the pain and corruption of this world. In the moment of choice, I want and intend to obey God. How I praise Him that once I do surrender, Christ fills me with love, light, and peace.

Making Sense of Reality

In reading the Bible, we simply cannot escape the fact that words have power and that their influence can be wielded for good or evil. Tanya's story provides us with a vivid example of this. And the book of Proverbs declares this truth concisely and forcefully:

> *Words kill, words give life;*
> *they're either poison or fruit — you choose. (18:21)*

You choose. That's what this book is about, right? Your choosing, and choosing wisely. To live the life you crave, important decisions about how you will receive and use words must be made.

Scripture also teaches that words reveal the heart that speaks them: "For whatever is in your heart determines what you say" (Matthew 12:34, NLT). Words give others a glimpse of who we truly are and what we're truly thinking.

Clearly, God sees words as a significant way to communicate one's inner being. In fact, John 1:1-14 refers to Jesus as *Logos*—the Word. Christ, the eternal Word incarnated, expresses the mind, character, and purpose of God. Through Jesus, *through the Word*, God gives us more than a glimpse of who He is: "No one has ever seen God. But God the only Son . . . has shown us what God is like" (John 1:18, NCV).

Through Jesus' life, God reveals that words help us make sense of reality. Jesus made sense of this world by being *"the Word,"* present in the world and speaking words into it. Through His teaching and His presence, Christ forever changed the way people understand the world around them.

In an amazing way, Jesus offers us the chance to participate in this eternal project. Through our words we, too, can make sense of reality and help others do the same. We can also, however, choose to disorder and confuse reality. But Scripture clearly reveals,

> *It's your heart, not the dictionary, that gives meaning to your words. . . . Let me tell you something: Every one of these careless words is going to come back to haunt you. There will be a time of Reckoning. Words are powerful; take them seriously. Words can be your salvation. Words can also be your damnation. (Matthew 12:34,36-37)*

Yikes! I don't know about you, but the thought that every one of my careless words will eventually come back to me, that there will be a reckoning and that my words can save or damn me, is more than a little unnerving.

Like Tanya, I learned early on that words can be weapons or shields. Jesus' command in Matthew 12 to *take words seriously* is a life-long challenge for many of us. To believe and live out the truths that words reveal our inner being, that our conversation can bring sense or chaos to our world, and that it's the heart — not the definition of the words themselves — that gives meaning to our speech, we must exercise great discernment.

Don't Ask, Don't Tell

I'd venture to guess that if you grew up in church, you've heard your share of talks about gossip. Some readers may be tempted to skip this section about gossip because they've "heard it all." But I sincerely hope you won't skim the following pages. I know I sometimes tune out certain subjects because I've never taken the time to *really* deal with them. And most of the time we don't thoughtfully examine the tone or content of our conversations.

No matter how much we've "learned" about gossip, we still talk about people without thinking. Despite the fact that many of us have heard this reasoning critiqued, we still believe that if everything we say is true, it can't be gossip. And depending on how Christian we feel on any given day, we may still use the worn-out and false excuse, "I was just sharing it so we could pray for so-and-so."

It's far easier to claim that we know God doesn't want us to gossip and go on with our daily lives than it is to admit that we've heard a lot of the truths but never chosen to apply them. When it comes to whether a piece of information or an entire conversation is slanderous, we desperately need discernment.

My desire is to look at gossip from a very practical, decision-focused angle. In order to do that, as we have seen in other chapters, we will benefit first and foremost from comparing what we think about gossip to what is actually true. As always, choosing how to set our minds is the beginning of discernment.

The Greek word for *gossip* is *diablos*, the same word from which we take our English word *devil*. *Diablos* means to accuse or misrepresent information. Closely related is the Greek word for *slander*, *blasphemia*, which means to speak evil of or to vilify, to malign or disparage. Our English word for the highest degree of slander is *blaspheme*, an approximate transliteration of the Greek *blasphemia*.[1] To blaspheme someone means to scornfully belittle or tear them apart with words.

Basically, this means gossip can be done inadvertently in the context of idle, careless chatter, while slander arises during the open and deliberate communication of potentially harmful information (whether true or false). Sadly, no matter what our intentions, gossip and slander result in the same widespread destruction.

Ouch! Not only does all of this sound painful and humiliating, but it also sounds a little too close for comfort—like some of the conversations I've heard and participated in. I think back on times when my friends and I verbally shredded someone with calculated ferocity. I remember times when I've accused others and even, as awful as it is to admit, times I've misrepresented information for my own advantage or to make a story sound juicier. And I recall moments when I've recognized—too late—that what came out of my mouth, though totally unpremeditated, could really hurt someone. To think that on those occasions I willingly sided with the Devil, the Accuser, terrifies and shames me.

Our God minces no words when He talks about gossip and slander. In James 3:8-10 He proclaims, "The tongue runs wild, a wanton killer. With our tongues we bless God our Father; with the same tongues we curse the very men and women he made in his image. Curses and blessings out of the same mouth! My friends, this can't go on."

The most important choice we can make about gossip and slander is to see them as they truly are—destructive, uncontrollable, and murderous. Now, that may initially sound a bit extreme, but think of how many reputations you've seen destroyed by vicious rumors. Think of the times you've been criticized behind closed doors. It's for good reason that the phrase "they stabbed me in the back" came into common parlance.

No wonder God commands us to take our words seriously. Our Father has watched as His precious sons and daughters have been maligned and vilified. He's seen their tears fall, their stomachs knot, their anger and resentment fester. He's also grieved as individuals or groups have attacked their neighbors, family members, or (former) friends. As we slander others He created to reflect and represent Him, it's *His* heart that breaks the most.

James 4:11 instructs, "Don't bad-mouth each other" and then vividly explains why: "It's God's Word, his Message, his Royal Rule, that takes a beating in that kind of talk. You're supposed to be honoring the Message, not writing graffiti all over it." Ultimately, gossip always defames God. Chances are, when the words, "Did you hear about . . ." or "I'm not sure if I should tell you this . . ." come out of your mouth, you're not trying to disparage God's holy name. But according to Scripture, that is precisely what happens. There's no arguing with His Word: All gossip eventually ends up directed at the throne of God.

Deciding to accept these fundamental truths begins the journey of discernment. But there are a few other aspects of gossip and slander that we must squarely face if we want to grow in discernment and start making wise choices.

First, gossip creates false intimacy. It fosters a perverse closeness between people "privileged" enough to share information. Being "in the know" can intoxicate people, making them feel special, included, accepted.

Second, a sense of empowerment also comes from evaluating and denigrating others. What's often behind comments like, "I can't believe they did that" or "I'm so sad that they . . ." is a self-satisfied smugness. We may be grateful that we haven't ended up "where they are," but when it accompanies gossip, this "gratitude" is *not* a positive, life-affirming thankfulness. More often it's a "Ha! I did something better than they did" sigh of relief.

And finally, recognizing that we're more prone to gossip when we've got little else to talk about is also important. Do you know anyone who seems to have nothing better to do than talk about other people? Joseph Stowell plainly said, "People who are constructively involved with their own [lives] have little time to be nosy about the [lives] of others."[2] In this simple but profound statement, we find one of the first decisions discernment can help us make. We can *choose* to have better things to do with our lives than gossip. We can *choose* to have more interesting things to talk about.

Of course, this may require something of us. We may need to trade slander for vulnerability (actually talking about our own struggles or thoughts). We may need to stop reading or watching things that promote gossip and start trying to stretch ourselves personally. As we grow, we have more to share about what God is teaching us.

We also may need to withdraw—temporarily or completely—from relationships in which gossip has become the norm. Becky, a girlfriend of mine, decided that though it would be extremely difficult for her, she just couldn't hang out with some of the other ladies from church. In fact, on one occasion she asked for their forgiveness because she'd engaged with them in what she *knew* was flat-out gossip (while standing outside the sanctuary on Sunday morning, no less). These "good Christian women" dismissed her comments with an "it's no big deal" attitude.

I've experienced some of the same. While leading a small-group discussion on judgmentalism, a twenty-something gal made the comment, "There's such a fine line between gossip and sharing. It's hard, you know?" In the midst of researching for this chapter, I couldn't agree. "I've learned the line isn't that fine," I replied. I explained that although it means talking less, listening more, and slowing down my wildfire conversation, God has really impressed on my heart that the Holy Spirit can and will *clearly* reveal whether my motives are pure or not.

Here's another practical decision we can make: Let's listen and obey rather than keep talking. I wonder if sometimes when we claim "it's hard to tell" whether we're gossiping or not, the real problem is that we've silenced the Spirit's voice on so many other occasions that our ears need retraining.

As a virtually incessant talker, I'm challenged by Proverbs 10:19; in fact, it's become one of my life verses:

> If you talk a lot, you are sure to sin;
>   if you are wise, you will keep quiet. (NCV)

These words might've been rendered, "Discerning people know how to restrain their words." As the New Living Translation puts it, they know when to "be sensible and turn off the flow."

We need not limit this advice to our own words. We can help others stop a barrage of gossip or slander. I like some of the direct but respectful phrases Stowell recommended in *The Weight of Your Words*. When we discern gossip is happening (or about to happen), he recommended we say, "Don't tell me. I already have more negative thoughts than I know what to do with." Or, if a friend starts with the infamous phrase, "You know, I really shouldn't be telling you this," we can deliberately choose not to respond with the standard, "Oh, come on, you can't stop now!" Try using this line instead; "Good for you. Don't tell me. I admire your self-control."[3]

Neither of these comments condemns the other person. And it's absolutely true that most people have enough negative thoughts to deal with. Perhaps affirming someone else's self-restraint will encourage us the next time we're confronted with the choice to either dive into or turn off the flow of gossip.

It's also easy to be led into gossip or slander when we think we've got our doctrine "right on" and someone else believes differently. In

1 Corinthians 10:28-31, Paul chronicled his personal experience with such slander. Other followers of the Way viciously tore the apostle apart because he ate meat sacrificed to idols.

Martha Peace made an excellent point in expounding on this passage for *Damsels in Distress*. She wrote clearly and simply, "While it's fine to have your own personal standards, it is not fine to unbiblically judge and slander others who do not hold to the same guidelines."[4] We can positively choose to let God guide those who decide differently than we do. Gossip and slander only tear down the immense and beautiful freedom of choice we've been given by God. This isn't to say that we should excuse clear violations of God's law. But in instances of obvious sin, the biblical rule of thumb is always to approach the offender directly (you can find the steps outlined in Matthew 18:15-17).

In matters of faith and freedom, God leaves no room for gossip or slander. Instead, He commands us to take the matter to Him, our faithful and just Judge, and to protect others by lovingly covering, rather than exposing, their shame.

In all things, "Let us then pursue what makes for peace and for mutual upbuilding" (Romans 14:19, NRSV). Just think, what would it be like if people chose to speak only when their words would edify and bring greater harmony to this hurting world?

Just Kidding

I'm not sure exactly when the transformation of common speech occurred, but the almost total dissolution of modern conversation into cynical and sarcastic banter is undeniable.

Of course, irony is certainly nothing new. Hundreds of years ago, some of my favorite novelists, like Jane Austen, used it with great and humorous results. Long before Austen, ancient Greeks and Romans, Chaucer, Shakespeare, Goethe (and the list goes on and on) utilized sarcasm to drive home their points, to expose the foolishness of certain characters, and to maintain the sense of tension and hilarity that irony so brilliantly promotes.

For some time, biting comments and derisive jokes were the territory of literary minds, those who could craft words with intelligence and wit. As people became exposed to these techniques of conversation, sarcasm was used in more intimate relationships—where there was either safety or a cruelly exploited vulnerability (as in Tanya's family)—to scorn and mock, often with the goal of making others laugh or cry.

But a far more widespread use of disdainful sarcasm can now readily be seen on screens big or small, read in mass media, and heard in nearly every conversation. Truly, "what would have raised red flags just a few years ago now raises smiles and rapt attention with perhaps only a little twinge of conscience. Marginal expressions, questionable jokes, and phrases with double meanings are tolerated and often enjoyed."[5]

Please don't misunderstand me: I'm not against irony. Irony can give life depth and reveal the humor in our often broken, topsy-turvy circumstances. God surely knows that we need and want to laugh. But now, more than ever, we need discernment to use irony appropriately. We cannot live our lives like a television sitcom, where practically all dialogue consists of cynical remarks tossed back and forth between characters who seem unfazed by the perpetual skirmishes of wit.

In real life, sarcasm can hurt people. In real life, too many people use sarcasm—as Tanya pointed out—to either wound others or defend themselves. In real life, too many people who don't want to be hurt or bothered with intimacy hide behind mockery, scorn, and derisive joking.

We cannot unthinkingly "go with the flow" of modern speech. While we don't have to chuck irony altogether, it's essential that we carefully consider our words. The apostle Peter summed this up in 1 Peter 3:8-9: "Be agreeable, be sympathetic, be loving, be compassionate, be humble. That goes for all of you, no exceptions. No retaliation.

No sharp-tongued sarcasm. Instead, bless—that's your job, to bless. You'll be a blessing and also get a blessing."

Discernment can help us make two important distinctions: when our sarcasm is, as Peter calls it, "sharp-tongued," and whether or not we are keeping with our primary job, to bless others. While it certainly can be a gift—a blessing—to make people laugh, wisely discerning when our words will cut and when they will build up is extremely important.

English speakers derived the word *sarcasm* from the Greek terms *sarkasmós* and *sarkázein*, which mean "to rend." It's no mistake that people refer to sarcastic comments as "cutting remarks." The very origin of the word implies that cynical humor intends to rip its target apart.

Webster's dictionary uses words such as *harsh, sharp, bitter,* and *sardonic* to define *sarcasm* and *cynicism*. I found it particularly illuminating that the word *sardonic* alludes to a plant native to the Mediterranean island Sardinia which, when eaten, supposedly produces convulsive laughter ending in death.

Without discernment, though lethal humor may not be our design, cutting and cynical jokes can spread the stench of death into our minds and relationships. This is the sharp-tongued sarcasm that Peter commanded us to avoid.

It's essential to consider whether our "funny" comments shame others, exposing their weaknesses or passions in order to mock them. Shame is a force of almost unparalleled toxicity. Because it attacks the very core of who we are, draining us of our dignity and confidence, the existential writer Jean-Paul Sartre rightly termed shame "an internal hemorrhage" of the soul.[6]

Almost every human questions at one time or another, *Does God actually love me unconditionally, or will He turn away in disgust when He sees me as I really am?* We also wonder, *What about other people? Would they care about me if they knew what I think, what I do, who I really am?* Shame makes it virtually impossible to answer these questions positively. Shame says, "There's something fundamentally wrong with you, something that you can't control or change."

And the trouble with sarcasm is that it often touches on these deep fears. We've all experienced the anxieties of being excluded, ridiculed, and revealed for the "nothings" we sometimes suspect we are. We've all feared being shamed. Theologian Lewis Smedes offered one of the best and most heartbreakingly vivid definitions of shame I've come across. He wrote,

> Shame is a vague, undefined heaviness that presses on our spirit, dampens our gratitude for the goodness of life, and slackens the free flow of joy. Shame is a primal feeling, the kind that seeps into and discolors all our other feelings, primarily about ourself but about almost everyone and everything else in our life as well.[7]

Now, we may not always intend our sarcastic comments to shame others. But part of the journey of discernment is recognizing that we bear some responsibility for the way our words affect others. With our words, we are ever pushing one another to become more beautiful or more broken.

Tragically, sarcasm has pervaded casual conversation so completely that we don't even stop to consider whether our humor will help or hurt. We toss comments around pretty carelessly, wouldn't you say? But as these powerful words from Ecclesiastes 5:6 teach us, God holds us accountable for every word, no matter how unintentionally spoken:

> Don't let your mouth make a total sinner of you.
> When called to account, you won't get by with
>   "Sorry, I didn't mean it."

Over a decade ago, the story of a Norwegian teenager who burned down his school shocked people around the world. The young man decided to celebrate the end of school by torching his books. Unfortunately, he set his backpack bonfire a bit too close to a storage shed, which happened to be just close enough to the school to ignite an uncontrollable blaze. One careless choice, and an entire school went up in flames.[8]

In the same way, our thoughtlessly made and sarcastic jokes often burn. "It only takes a spark," James 3:5-7 reminds us, "to set off a forest fire. A careless or wrongly placed word out of your mouth can do that. By our speech we can ruin the world, turn harmony to chaos, throw mud on a reputation, send the whole world up in smoke and go up in smoke with it, smoke right from the pit of hell. This is scary." Yeah, it is. It's horrifying to think that we can ruin the world and turn harmony into chaos through our words. Sarcasm can be *far more* dangerous than we realize. We need to choose wisely when to use it and when to restrain ourselves. Otherwise, we risk sending the work of God up in smoke — "smoke right from the pit of hell."

I wish I could offer you a surefire formula to avoid sharp-tongued sarcasm and use irony only in appropriate ways. But the personal and circumstantial nature of words (how they change based on the tone and intention of a given instance) makes this impossible.

There are, however, two guidelines that have helped me. Evelyn Underhill offered one in the form of a prayer: "May I never take such words on my lips, O Lord, that I could not pass directly from them to the hallowing of Your name." Diligently applying this one principle over a lifetime, Underhill noted, would establish peace and grace at the center of any heart.[9]

If I were to actually evaluate whether all of my "just kidding" comments could lead to a hallowing of God's name, I know I'd have to leave some out (probably far more than I'd like to admit in print). But analyzing how we use sarcasm provides an amazing opportunity for us to draw close to the Holy Spirit, close enough to hear His still, small voice. God will tell us when to hold our tongues and when to bless instead of curse, even in jest.

The other guideline we can use is whether our sarcasm encourages people to think purely and positively about God and each other. If we truly hold our conversation up to the Light, we may find that our speech communicates shame or contempt, cynicism, or sexual inappropriateness.

As I indicated previously, while researching for this chapter, I found it incredibly enlightening to look at various meanings of sarcasm, cynicism, and irony. I found "disparaging the motives or sincerity of others" among Webster's definitions of cynical.[10] A cynic can be defined as someone who believes only selfishness motivates human actions and therefore cannot believe that love, goodness, beauty, or any other virtue might compel someone. Vicious skepticism often results. Pessimism and distrust of other people pervade so much of our world already. Surely we don't need to contribute to this general mode of conversation, which tends toward contempt, scorn, and self-protection.

I also discovered that cynicism and sarcasm involve "showing contempt for accepted standards of honesty or morality, especially by actions that exploit the scruples of others."[11] Sarcastic comments, even when intended for "innocent" jest, often mock, downplay, or ridicule the convictions of another person. Sometimes our remarks border on sneering contempt for the standards of God Himself.

I'll give you an example from my life, one I'm not particularly proud to confess. While interviewing Rob, a potential staff member for the high school department at our church, one of the other leaders asked what he thought about dating. He responded that his experience involved only one relationship. Rob started to say, "It lasted a year and—" But before he could continue, I blurted out something like, "and it was with a guy, so that had to end."

Everyone around the table laughed. I remember Rob played right into my sarcastic comment, but to this day I couldn't tell you what he said. I felt so convicted, so immediately, that it nearly took my breath away. It was as if the Holy Spirit asked me, *Would it really be funny if Rob was gay?* I've had several very good friends who have chosen or battled against homosexuality. It's not a laughing matter. The Spirit revealed to me that my comment not only cut Rob down (though he didn't seem bothered), but also made a joke of God's standards.

Sharing this story with you, I run the risk of some people throwing their hands up in frustration: "Give me a break! It was just a joke." Yes, it was. And because I don't have a corner on the "what God finds funny" market, I'm willing to concede. There may be times when humor about sexual orientation doesn't bother God; however, even if there are such times, this was *not* one of them.

My experience that day helped me see two things about sarcasm that I'd like you to think about. First, how our words are received at the time is not the only indicator of whether we used irony appropriately or not. Remember, everyone around me that day laughed; no one else seemed to skip a beat. Second, sarcasm and sexual innuendo often link themselves together in a rather precarious way. Ask yourself: Do you ever use sarcasm to get away with comments about sex or relationships that you wouldn't dare state forthrightly?

Again, all of the questions this book brings up are meant to spark conversation between you and God. *He* is the Source of all wisdom and discernment. The Spirit will direct if you'll allow Him to.

Becoming Color-Blind

Let's look together now at God's direction for one more area: how discernment helps us avoid manipulative and deceitful communication.

Dr. Samuel Johnson, eighteenth-century scholar and author of the first great English dictionary, once claimed, "Men are like stone jugs—you may lug them where you like by their ears." I'll be the first to admit that I like to get what I want. And I've often been guilty of getting what I want by manipulating my words (or how someone will take my words).

Because this is a practice common to many of us, I felt it extraordinarily important that we discuss how discernment can help us avoid manipulative speech and its close companion, deceit. Manipulation and deceit can take many forms. Exaggeration is perhaps one of the most frequently employed methods since its purposes can span from the relatively innocent goal of adding entertainment value to more pernicious motives for personal gain. Other forms of manipulation like sweet talk or begging aim at overriding the judgment and will of people around us. The phrase "I talked them into it" implies you decided what you wanted and used words to get it (often no matter what the cost).

Rather than respecting people and allowing them to make up their own minds, we often try to push one another to do what *we* want, when *we* want it. But Jesus exposed the folly of influencing the decisions of others through manipulative ploys. Tucked in His brilliant and challenging Sermon on the Mount, Jesus made a seemingly simple comment, which actually takes many of us a lifetime to learn: "Just say 'yes' and 'no.' When you manipulate words to get your own way, you go wrong" (Matthew 5:37).

When we use tearful or angry words ("If you really loved me you'd . . ."), when we withdraw our words and give the cold shoulder, when we accuse or threaten ("If you don't _____, I don't know what I'll do")[12] to manipulate someone into doing what we want, we just plain *go wrong.*

Though it may not be an experiment you're excited to perform, I challenge you to take a week to evaluate how often you stray from the exact truth when relating a story, asking for a favor, or having a disagreement. Look carefully at how you may use (or even be tempted to use) manipulative ploys to get your way.

Discerning the ways we tend toward manipulation is an important first step in deciding to live by God's clear command to "put away from you crooked speech, and put devious talk far from you" (Proverbs 4:24, NRSV).

An essential second step comes in discerning what to do when someone else is manipulating us. I appreciate what Martha Peace observed in her book *Damsels in Distress*: "When someone is manipulating you, you are likely to have very unpleasant emotions—fear, confusion, frustration, or guilt. So your emotions will make it difficult for you to respond without sinning (defending yourself, blowing up in anger, sinfully giving in)."[13] In other words, the emotions we feel when being manipulated often cause us to resort to manipulative ploys of our own. Peace goes on to draw a clear comparison between manipulative people and the fools Proverbs describes. The Bible teaches us, "When arguing with fools, don't answer their foolish arguments, or you will become as foolish as they are" (Proverbs 26:4, NLT).

Discerning people will recognize when attempted (or semi-successful) manipulation has been used against them. They may decide to take a step back or even to postpone the conversation until another time. If you suspect you're being manipulated, there's nothing wrong with choosing to say, "I'd like to think about what you've said and how to respond. Can we come back to this later?"

In the heat of a conversation, when someone is sweet-talking or begging you, threatening or accusing you, tearfully or angrily ranting against you, it can become very difficult to hear the Holy Spirit's voice. And when *you're* using these ploys, you can silence the conviction of the Spirit inside you. In these instances, discernment can help you decide to back away and take the matter to God for clear direction.

You can also ask Him to bring it to your attention the next time you start down the path of deceit or manipulation. As soon as possible, stop your conversation and take a moment to confess this to the Lord (even if you're out shopping with a friend, you can duck into the ladies' room for two minutes). He will show you what to do next.

Here's the problem, though: We want instant results. When we call a friend to ask if she can watch our kids or needy pet while we go out for the night, we don't really want her to respond, "Let me pray about it and I'll get back to you." We want to have things settled. We may be tempted to use a phrase such as, "I don't know who else to call; you're the only one I can really count on" to make our friend feel special and sort of, though we hope not in an altogether negative way, obligated to do us the favor.

When we're on the other side of the equation, we usually want to please rather than disappoint our friends. We may not want to take time to listen for God's direction because we're afraid to let our friends down.

Add to this the fact that most people find it rather easy to slip into deceptive comments that "protect" others or themselves from the real truth. When a friend asks, "Why didn't you call me back?" we may feel defensive and claim, "I tried to reach you all day, but I got a busy signal." In reality, we called twice, but "tried to reach you all day" certainly sounds as if we made a more concentrated effort.

Though completely unpremeditated, when someone asks us, "Have you done _____ yet?" we may instinctively and automatically stretch the truth to protect our reputation and our relationship. We think a deceitful comment will be just enough to keep the other person happy and us safe, so we respond with, "Yes. I'm taking care of it."

I'm annoyed and ashamed at how quickly I can exaggerate, manipulate, or deceive to get my way or to protect myself. Discernment helps me see my ploys for what they sometimes are: lies.

In writing about deceit and manipulation in *The Weight of Your Words*, Joseph Stowell made an incredibly important observation. He wrote, "Lying is the strength of Satan's system. Not only does he lie, but his desire is that we will lie as well. When we lie, we imitate Satan rather than God."[14] That says it pretty clearly, doesn't it? We'll always be tempted to lie, deceive, and manipulate because that's our Enemy's primary strategy. We must choose, and keep on choosing, to side with the God of Truth rather than the father of lies (see John 8:44).

Discernment helps us analyze our words with unflinching diligence. It helps us see clearly and accurately. A wise person once declared, "People given to white lies soon become color-blind."

Lord, may we never lose sight of what is true and good.

A Priority Skill

Whether developing your abilities as a gymnast or carpenter, you must first master certain priority skills before progressing to more difficult things. In order to throw a full twist, a gymnast should have a solid round-off back handspring. To bevel a table, a woodworker needs to be more than competent with certain tools and techniques.

Priority skills enable us to master other things with greater ease and dexterity. As our ability to execute priority skills increases, related practices come much more naturally.

Using words with discernment is a priority skill for life. If you want to live well, learning to speak and receive words appropriately should be a top priority.

Avoiding gossip, blessing others rather than cutting them down, and steering clear of manipulation and deceit are three aspects that consistently call for our discernment. Of course, there are many other dimensions to words that challenge our decision-making ability (how and why we make promises, when we rebuke or encourage, why we praise, and so on).

But I think focusing on gossip, sarcasm, and manipulation has given us plenty to think about for now. Let's take some time to discuss and meditate, asking God to solidify what we've learned and translate it into practical application.

Questions for Discussion

1. Talk or journal about the following story from the Middle Ages: A young man approaches a monk and confesses, "I've sinned by telling slanderous tales about someone. What should I do?" The man of God replies, "Put a feather on every doorstep in town." Glad for such an easy penance, the young man does just that. But when he returns to the monk, wondering if there's anything else he should do, the man of God commands him, "Go back and pick up all those feathers." Startled, the young man exclaims, "That's impossible! By now the wind will have blown them all over town!" Says the monk, "So have your slanderous words become impossible to retrieve."[15] Can you recall a time when you either gossiped about someone or were gossiped about? What emotions does this memory stir up in you? Is there anyone you need to forgive or ask forgiveness of? Take a moment to sit silently with the Holy Spirit, asking Him to show you how discernment might help you the next time you're in a similar situation.

2. What do you think about the story I related in our exploration of sarcasm (the one in which I joked about a fellow youth worker's sexual orientation)? Revisit that account with the following words from Scripture in mind: "Don't be flip with the sacred. Banter and silliness give no honor to God. Don't reduce holy mysteries to slogans. In trying to be relevant, you're only being cute and inviting sacrilege" (Matthew 7:6).

3. Why do you suppose people are so prone to manipulation and deception in their speech? How might we encourage one another to let go of the ploys we've often used to get our way?

Thoughts for Personal Meditation

What is most difficult for you about the following prayer?

> *Father, help me put these things out of my life: anger, bad temper, doing or saying things to hurt others, and using evil words when I talk. Help me not to lie to, manipulate, or deceive others. I have left my old sinful life and the things I did before. I praise You that I have begun to live the new life in which I am being made new and am becoming like You. Mold me in this new life more each day. Amen. (Adapted from Colossians 3:8-10, NCV)*

Talk to God about the challenges that lie before you and ask for the help He is ready to give.

A Prayer to Spark Your Conversation with God

You can say many times throughout the day this simple prayer from the Psalms, which sums up most everything discussed in this chapter:

> *Lord, help me control my tongue;*
> > *help me be careful about what I say. (141:3, NCV)*

FIVE

Beyond Distraction

WHERE DISCERNMENT AND YOUR RESOURCES INTERSECT

YOU WOULD LOVE MY girlfriend Kara. She's witty, winsome, and wild in the best kind of way. She knits amazingly beautiful scarves, cooks like a gourmet, and always has something interesting to say. That's probably because she reads incessantly—everything from historical nonfiction to theology to Agatha Christie and Dorothy Sayers mysteries. Kara's love of music recently prompted her to take up the guitar, though she did candidly confess, "It's not going all that well." Apparently, no matter how much you adore music, strumming chord patterns is a lot more difficult than it looks.

When Kara's not practicing music or reading a book, stirring some phenomenal sauce or taking a long walk with a friend, she likes to shop at thrift stores. "Even if I don't buy anything," she admitted to me a couple of days ago, "I like to *think* about buying things. I guess that's pretty bad, isn't it?" "It doesn't have to be," I laughingly replied. "But I'm fascinated. Why would you say that, Kara?"

So much of what Kara and I discussed in response to that question fit perfectly with this book. I wanted to let you in on my conversation with Kara as we continue the journey of discernment into a very personal, potentially feather-ruffling area: how we choose to spend our free time.

What Reality Are You Escaping To?

"I think we all need a break sometimes," Kara continued. "And I know there's nothing inherently wrong with shopping. But for me, there are times when I purposefully buy, or allow myself to dwell on what I would buy, because I don't want to deal with real life. It's the same reason I gave up TV and Christian romance novels in college."

"What?" I asked.

"I stopped watching TV and reading romantic books for a long stretch," Kara answered, "because I felt convicted; I was spending too much time trying to escape reality. It wasn't like I heard a voice from heaven, but I knew God was directing me to surrender them, you know?"

"I do know," I said. "That's happened to me with different things. Was it hard for you?"

"Sure. I had started reading Christian romance novels in my early teens. My grandma was crazy about them. She used to preview them and give me what she called the cutest, cleanest ones. But as God started prompting me to stop reading even those books, I clearly saw that I used them — maybe not all the time, but certainly some of the time — to fill a void that I needed to allow God to fill instead."

"What do you mean?" I asked.

"Well, I never dated in high school. Novels let me feel some romance in what seemed like an innocent way. But in college, when the desire for a boyfriend became more intense, the books were definitely a way for me to escape and live out a 'safe' fantasy — totally clean and

Christian, but still a reality that wasn't my own.

"And I could justify reading them because, again, there's nothing wrong with mentally 'getting away' for a while every now and then. This question kept coming up in my mind, though: What reality am I escaping to?"

"So how did you answer that?" I wanted to know.

"I didn't at first. It took me almost a year to do what God was asking me to do—give up the novels, I mean. There didn't seem to be a specific reason God wanted me to surrender them, and there wasn't anything bad about the books, so I just kept ignoring the feelings, the questions inside me. But the topics of listening to God and making good choices kept coming up in sermons and other things I was reading. Finally I decided that even if God wasn't writing His directions on the wall, He *was* speaking to me. I chose to let the books go and not keep trying to justify them."

"What happened?"

"Well, the busyness of college distracted me plenty, and there was a lot of other great stuff out there to read. But then my grandmother died and left me a bunch of her old novels. I missed her, and they reminded me of her, so I picked the books up again, figuring that I had 'fasted' from them long enough."

"Had you?" I asked. "Fasted from them long enough?"

Kara laughed. "Apparently not. In fact, at that point I was twenty-four and had an even deeper longing for romantic love and a husband and all that goes with that. The novels touched on these basic needs and desires, but they didn't help the ache go away. In some ways it got stronger."

"So what did you do?"

"Nothing at first. Again I justified my choices. They were *just books*, for crying out loud. My goodness, I thought to myself, didn't lots of my good Christian friends read them? Didn't everyone say I analyze things too much anyway? Wasn't I entitled to a little mindless fluff now and then?

"But this was the thing, Jerusha: I was — and *am* — working so hard to stay pure, not just in a sexual way, but also spiritually. Sometimes I'm frustrated out of my mind, though, and it's very tempting to get a release through something so seemingly innocent."

Kara leaned in suddenly, clearly about to tell me something that shocked her. "Do you know they offer a stripping class at Bally's Total Fitness? One of my friends is thinking about taking it. To express her sexuality, she says. It's as if she thinks, 'I'm not stripping for real, so there's nothing wrong with it.' To some people, taking a teach-you-to-tease class may seem more extreme than my clean Christian romance novels, but her justifications and motivations sounded pretty darn close to my own. That kind of unnerves me."

I sat there thinking about the times I've similarly justified the things I do (or want to do) in my spare time — the movies I've watched, the time I've spent on the Web daydreaming about vacations or possessions, lured away by the empty promises of "entertainment value."

"Look," Kara continued. "I'm still trying to figure out what it means to be holy — mind, body, and spirit. And the options to take a strip class or watch borderline-lewd TV (you know the shows I mean) or buy stuff because I've been working my tail off and want to reward myself or even read Christian novels that make me unhealthily long for something I don't have all bring into sharper focus this question: What reality am I escaping to?

"We all need or want to get some space from the hard things in life, but to take that space, to escape reality, without thinking is dangerous. It just becomes clearer and clearer as I get older: Every decision is sacred, and every choice, no matter how small, has repercussions."

By this time I knew I wanted to use some of Kara's comments in this chapter on discernment and free time. So I asked Kara point-blank, "If you could communicate one thing to other people who want to honor God with their time and activities, what would it be?"

"Oh, I got it!" Kara exclaimed. She grabbed her Bible and read 1 Corinthians 10:23: "'All things are lawful,' but not all things are beneficial. 'All things are lawful,' but not all things build up" (NRSV). Then Kara gave me her interpretation of the verse: "God ultimately gives us the freedom to do what we want. But just because you and I are free doesn't make decision making unimportant. Pretending that our choices don't matter is self-deception. I may have been free to watch "that" movie, for instance, but to ask, 'Was it beneficial (helpful, valuable, constructive, positive)?' opens a different dimension of responsibility.

"More often than not, I grew up doing—or not doing—things because of something my parents or a leader at church told me. But I've seen that not thinking for yourself can be just as treacherous as carelessly doing whatever you please. To live well, we have to *think* and *choose*. I've learned that to live the fullest life, I have to be intentional," Kara concluded.

And I say "Amen" to that.

When You Don't Have to Do Anything

In his exceptional book *A Long Obedience in the Same Direction*, pastor and Bible translator Eugene Peterson made a very simple yet profound observation: "An excellent way to test [our] values is to observe what we do when we don't have to do anything, how we spend our leisure time, how we spend our extra money."[1]

I tend to think of myself as having no leisure time and no extra money. I've got two young children, I'm a pastor's wife, and I work part-time. My family lives in a hyperexpensive part of Southern California, and when I think "extra money," images of the country-club set in Rancho Santa Fe come to mind.

Kara is five years younger than me, single, and without kids. Because our lives are pretty different, I asked Kara about her free time: "How many hours do you and friends at your same stage of life spend on media (TV, music, movies, books, magazines, newspapers, or the Internet) every day?"

After taking a minute to think, Kara replied, "On average, I'd say about three hours. Depending on what we've got going on, whether we're off or working that day. All of us apportion our time differently —we've each got a favorite media that we spend more time on and stuff we do only now and then. But I'd say three hours a day is a pretty good estimate. Don't get me started on my guy friends who play video games, though."

Three hours sounded like a lot to me. Again, I tend to think of myself as having no free time. But then I started counting. Even if I just watched a half hour of TV, listened to music to and from work, surfed the Web for a couple of things, answered some e-mails, and read a chapter or two in a book, that would easily make three hours. I might do less some days and more others, but I guess three hours isn't out of the ballpark for me either. Claiming that I have no free time and no extra money just doesn't hold water. I may have less free time now than I did at other stages of my life, but I do in fact have time for leisure, time during which I can choose what to do. The same is true of my money.

I wonder (and am a bit frightened to imagine) what you would determine my priorities are if the only information available to you was a survey of the ways in which I've spent my free time and money over the last fifteen years.

You might discover that I value encouraging people, as I spend part of my free time nearly every day writing notes or e-mails to people I love, want to thank, or desire to build up. You might learn that I enjoy a broad range of diverse pastimes, from reading philosophical nonfiction to scrapbooking. Perhaps you would conclude from these observations that I value engaging my mind and cherishing family memories.

But you surely would see other things as well. The Lord only knows (and grieves with me over) how many hours I've spent working out over the last fifteen years. The past seven years I've chosen to consciously restrict my exercise time because during the five before that, I obsessed not only about working out but also about eating or not eating certain things and at certain times. I shudder to imagine how much free time I've squandered thinking about calories, fat grams, and number of strides or how much money I've shelled out on low-carb, reduced-calorie, and fat-burning foods.

You likely would notice how often I've used movies (not so much TV, but sometimes that, too) to veg out after a stressful day or when other things—like facing my midterms, doing that mountain of dishes, or playing a third round of Princess Uno with my eager five-year-old—seemed tedious and overwhelming. Sometimes it's a whole lot easier to be entertained than it is to engage with life.

After looking at a report of how I've spent my free time and money over the last fifteen years, I wonder how much you would say I value being distracted from the wearying craze or tiresome monotony of normal life.

How often do you want to escape reality—the boredom, the drudgery, the dailiness of it all?

At twenty years old, I not only detested being bored, I was terrified of it. I also hated being silent or still because what I saw and felt in myself during those times seemed intolerable. So I entertained and busied myself in many ways, sometimes even using God as a distraction. Christian philosopher Blaise Pascal once explained my condition perfectly: "Nothing is so unbearable to a man as to be completely at rest, without passions, without business, without diversion, without study. He then feels his nothingness, his falseness, his insufficiency, his dependence, his weakness, his emptiness."[2]

By its nature, our "entertain me," "make me feel good" society is committed to what Pascal calls diversion, to activity that performs—before everything else—the anesthetic function of quieting our anguish. The tragedy of such diversion is that it distracts us from what is most immediate and authentic and *real* to us: the naked state of our hearts. Constantly being diverted keeps us from feeling our achingly desperate need for true joy, true fulfillment, true pleasure—in short, all the things that are found only in God.

I am now thirty-one years old. I don't feel the same discomforting fear I did at twenty of being alone with my thoughts or having nothing to do. But if I were to evaluate honestly how I currently spend my free time and money, I'm sure I'd still see ways in which I try to fill my emptiness and escape my falseness.

I'd also see the ways I try to justify particular decisions I make about spending leisure time or resources. I don't take an hour doing my makeup or hair in the morning, so the thirty-five minutes I spend on the elliptical machine seems short. When I've had a hard day, grabbing a Starbucks as a treat or flipping on a movie instead of playing with my kids doesn't seem that bad.

And it isn't—as long as I recognize that these are decisions I'm making, not rights or obligations or things I deserve. It's a *choice* to spend my time working out instead of doing something else. On any given day, I may make better or worse decisions than someone else, but how I spend my free time and resources always comes down to my *choice*. It's my *choice* to treat myself to something after a hard day. It's my *choice* to get lost for an hour on the Web looking at shoes.com. And what comes with every choice? That's right—consequences.

So often we fail to recognize the enormous freedom we have in determining how to spend our time and money. Instead, we make all kinds of mini-choices that sap our energy and resources and then lament that we have no free time and no extra money.

This is an extraordinarily difficult topic to discuss because I'm confident that some people will misread me. Someone is probably already upset that I said something about choosing to take time on your hair in the morning or that I'm not a big fan of TV. Please don't misunderstand me. I'm *not* trying to identify specifically right or wrong ways to spend your spare time and money. That is the *last* thing I'd be equipped or excited to do. I'm just trying to get all of us to recognize that we constantly — and a lot of times unthinkingly — make decisions about our free time and resources.

Discerning the best ways for you to spend your time would be impossible for me (and believe me, I'm grateful that's true because I don't want to be the one to schedule or rearrange your time!). What you and I can do together is hone our God-given skills of discernment so that when blessed with free time and/or money, we've got what it takes to make wise choices. Candidly discussing the great freedom we have in choosing how to apportion our energy and finances will help us make wise decisions, decisions we won't feel the need to justify or excuse or act as if they don't matter.

As with every other area we've explored, we'll start by looking at how we think and begin the process of reordering our perspectives. We've started the discussion a bit already, but let's focus more intently on why we choose certain activities when we don't *have* to do anything.

A Question Worth Pondering

After my talk with Kara, I spent a good deal of time thinking about a question she and I never answered together. I'd considered the truth that I sometimes use entertainment to escape reality. But I usually focused on identifying and then facing what I was trying to get away *from*, not evaluating what I tended to run *to*. It's a fascinating and important question, isn't it? What reality do we escape *to* in our spare time?

I tend to flee to a world where everything works out. Even if the heroine overcomes tremendous odds, nine times out of ten I want a book or movie that ends with a relatively believable "happily ever after."

I also tend to prefer a world where some people don't count on or matter to me. A few years ago, I felt convicted to stop watching a particular reality TV show because I found myself gossiping about the individuals on the show as if they were fictional characters, not real people. Like Kara, I could've justified my actions in every which way (and I did for a while). But when it boiled down, I saw that I liked judging and criticizing people supposedly without consequences.

And that brings up another aspect of the type of world I like to escape to: one without direct cause and effect. Sometimes I want to be able to "safely" imagine myself doing things (for example, feeling the tension before a first kiss) that I can't in real life.

In the real world, and stretching into eternity, it doesn't matter a *whit* that I won't have a first kiss again. What matters in real life is that I lovingly treasure the amazing gifts God's given me in my husband and children and that I keep myself for them. And I want to—with all my heart.

But sometimes when reading a book or watching a movie, I allow myself to vicariously experience dramatic, passionate, dangerous, or daring emotions and situations that don't build up my family or my faith. It's not that *every* time I pick up a book, flip on the tube, or go to the movies I'm trying to escape to a consequence-free life where people don't matter to me and everything's going to work out. Often I can enjoy entertainment in a more healthy way. And discernment helps me differentiate between the occasions I use free time well and those I don't.

Author and teacher Dallas Willard is right: Of all the things we can do, we have more freedom in regard to what we will think of and where we will focus our minds than we do with *anything else*. Quite simply, what occupies our everyday thoughts governs—in large part—what we do. It sets the emotional tone from which our choices spring, and it projects the options for action available to us in the future.[3] For some of us, that's a startling reality and a huge wake-up call.

What I think about in the free moments I have *every* day shapes how I feel about my life, the people around me, even God. It may not definitively determine what I do (watching a movie that includes adultery has never compelled me to want or pursue an affair), but it does set an emotional tone out of which my actions flow.

For instance, I can become quickly dissatisfied with my real life when I read about or watch a falsely romanticized marriage that works out perfectly (even if the obstacles to overcome were initially great). Though my husband is a wonderful man and Christian, I cannot control Jeramy's dialogue or actions like the author of a novel can. He is a real and flawed person, just like me. And we cannot see the earthly end of our story. We both believe in an eternal "happily ever after" with Jesus, but neither of us knows what sufferings this life may bring.

Watching TV and movies that titillate me through innuendo-laced sarcasm or that portray senseless brutality can also desensitize me to the crude comments and wicked violence that is *very present* in the world. Is being entertained by characters bantering about sex or seeing homicide cases glorified profitable?

Like Kara, I've determined that I cannot read every kind of book or watch every kind of movie. Some take me to mental and emotional places that I just don't need to go. I have an extremely vivid and easily unleashed imagination. I have to know myself and make choices based on accurate self-knowledge. For example, I am extremely sensitive to media that depicts violence against women. I can barely hear the theme song to *CSI* without picturing some horrific rape or murder scene. Images from horror movies I watched as a teenager sometimes resurface in my mind, haunting me to this day.

One of my best friends loves criminal novels. Of course, I don't know what goes on in her mind, but it *genuinely* seems like she can read them without being negatively affected. I cannot. Again, I know this about myself and have chosen to stay away from them, no matter how popular forensics TV shows, movies, books, or websites might be.

Candidly and mercilessly evaluating yourself is a big first step in discerning how you will and will not spend your free resources (time, energy, money). Ask yourself, *What thoughts, emotions, and actions spring up before, during, and after engaging in a particular activity (reading "that" book, watching "that" show or movie, being on "that" site)?*

I know it's not a good idea for me to browse online shopping sites, but not for the reason you might initially suspect. I'm not so much tempted to overbuy as I am to feel discouraged or frustrated that I don't have more money. It's difficult enough to "be done with . . . jealousy" (as 1 Peter 2:1, NLT, commands us to do). I don't need to add to the feelings of dissatisfaction and longing already within me. Perhaps you don't feel the way I do. Maybe you're tempted to spend more than you should. Maybe you don't have an issue with browsing at all.

The important thing, rather than getting caught up in the specifics of what anyone else can or can't do, is to honestly discern (distinguish between, judge, determine, perceive) what activities are best for *you* and which *you* would do well to avoid. I bring up the differences between us only to reemphasize the unique and personal nature of discernment.

At this point, I'd like to acknowledge that there may be some readers out there thinking, *Give me a break. Why do you have to make it this complicated? Evaluating everything seems overboard to me.* This is how I would reply to anyone who thinks I'm being extreme: We expend the same energy one way or another. We spend our time either afterward, digesting and then dealing with the things we've impulsively and indiscriminately consumed, or beforehand, preserving and protecting ourselves because we are worth it and, more important, *God is worth it.*

If your best friend's wedding was tomorrow and you knew that eating a particular food (or too much of it) might make you sick, I'd venture to guess that you'd steer clear. You'd want to be present and healthy because you love your friend. Sure, you might not get ill. But the risk isn't worth it.

So often we carelessly read, watch, and play around with virtually everything, believing the lie that "it doesn't affect me." Yet we wonder why feelings of lust, envy, anger, or disillusionment plague us.

The health and strength of our minds, bodies, and souls are worth the energy it takes to analyze what we will and will not do in our free time. If we decide to discern, we do what is best for ourselves. And even more significant, as we choose to evaluate what we will or will not do, we offer God our very best. He deserves no less.

Step by Step

But how do we actually go about evaluating what and what not to do? Are there any practical helps we can turn to? Absolutely! Remember the verse Kara read to us earlier? "'All things are lawful,' but not all things are beneficial.' All things are lawful,' but not all things build up" (1 Corinthians 10:23, NRSV). The New Century Version renders this verse, "'We are allowed to do all things,' but not all things are good for us to do."

It may sound simple, but authentically answering questions like the following will help us discern what to keep and what to avoid:

- Is this positive?
- Does this build up?
- Is this good for me to do (rather than just okay, something I have the right or freedom to do but is not really *good* for me)?

Most of the time we don't bother to consider these questions, so we're surprised that answers come when we actually ask them.

Quite simply, there are loads of books, movies, music, and products that we needn't read, see, listen to, or buy. If we wish, we certainly have the right to consume any of these media. But remember, a good deal of what cannot be called evil still is not good for us.

"And now, dear brothers and sisters, let me say one more thing. . . . Fix your thoughts on what is true and honorable and right. Think about things that are pure and lovely and admirable. Think about things that are excellent and worthy of praise." Obviously these aren't my words. They come straight from Philippians 4:8 (NLT). But what Paul encouraged his beloved friends ages ago, God also speaks to you and me.

People talk about "mindless" TV, movies, books, or Web surfing, but the reality is that *everything* engages our mind on some level. We subconsciously digest a lot more than we realize when we "tune out" to be entertained. We may be tempted, for instance, to excuse watching a particular movie (one that isn't honorable or pure) because "we don't *usually* think about those kinds of things." But the truth is that we just spent two hours of our life dwelling on them. And we do this over and over again.

Unfortunately we tend to see our free-time choices as disconnected from one another. What we watched six months ago has nothing to do with what we'll rent this weekend, right?

Wrong.

Our choices build on one another. *It's just one show*, we reason. But it's a different show every other night. *It's just one more shirt*, we rationalize. But we forget that when we see the perfect jeans and purse to go with it. *This movie isn't as bad as that one*, we think, *so it's okay if I watch it. This site isn't as provocative as that one, so if I just avoid the really bad stuff, I'll be okay.*

This may sound a bit harsh, but why are we (who want to be like Christ) constantly trying to live as close to the world as possible? We talk about wanting to be pure, but our choices show that what we *really* desire is to live on the outskirts of holiness, where we can still smell and taste and experience a bit of the world. Why?

Are we more concerned with fun than we are with anything else? Do we not think holiness will be pleasurable enough? Do we have any idea what real holiness—real "set-apartness"—would feel like? An even more penetrating question concerns who we are deep within: Beyond what we do or don't, beyond what we can or can't, what would we do *if we could get away with it?*[4]

I have to admit I don't have the perfect answers to these questions. And I certainly have been as guilty as others who have justified what they do in their spare time and with their spare money. But now more than ever, I want to press into the battle, not sit on the sidelines hoping only to be entertained.

During college I had a particularly disturbing experience in a Houston movie theater. I had joined a number of students headed to the opening-day matinee of a movie that critics were falling over themselves to praise. In one scene, a man accidentally gets shot at point-blank range. It's difficult to explain exactly how, but the situation is set up and directed to be humorous. Blood splattered, the audience roared, and I sat there, laughing at first and then completely stunned. For a brief moment, I saw myself and the hundred other people in the theater through another lens.

I knew God at the time, but I wasn't walking particularly close to Him. Still, I could feel the underlying tragedy of our amusement. A couple of years later when I read Thomas à Kempis's master work *The Imitation of Christ*, I recognized what I had been feeling: "We often indulge in empty laughter when we have good reason to weep."[5]

We can be so easily led to chuckle or smirk when we should rightly grieve at the brokenness—the glamorized promiscuity and adultery, the careless selfishness and vicious ambition, the mob violence and general wickedness—portrayed on our screens, in our books, and through our music. We have good reason to weep because these things are played out in our minds and in some people's lives. So many of us are, as Neil Postman titled his book twenty years ago, *Amusing Ourselves to Death*.

There's a deep connection between these things and our spiritual discontentment, too. If we choose not to fix our minds on what is true, excellent, pure, and honorable throughout the day, we find it much more difficult to center ourselves in prayer and meditation when we do go before God.

Brother Lawrence, the humble monk who authored one of the best-loved devotionals of all time, had it right: "One way to re-collect the mind easily in the time of prayer, and preserve it more in tranquility, is *not to let it wander too far at other times*. You should keep it strictly in the presence of God; and being accustomed to think of Him often, you will find it easy to keep your mind calm in the time of prayer, or at least to recall it from its wanderings." This Brother Lawrence called "practicing the presence of God" and deemed it "the best rule of a holy life."[6]

Indeed. If we desire to be genuinely set apart, we should consider how far we allow our minds to wander. I may *claim* that being in God's presence is my heart's desire, but do my choices, particularly my decisions concerning what to do with my leisure time and money, match with this declaration?

Not always . . .

Thankfully, though, that's not the end of the matter. Let me encourage you by filling in those ellipses.

Not always . . . and yet *more than they used to*.

There's a big difference between saying, "I'm not perfect" and stating, "Nothing has changed." Here on earth I'll never arrive, but I'm so grateful that as I wrestle with the questions, as I discern what really is beneficial and what does build up, God *does* transform me.

Until we are home with Jesus, our intentions and actions won't perfectly match. But we can, *you can*, be progressively renovated. And you *will* change as you determine—no matter what the cost to your "entertainment"—to honestly evaluate your choices against the biblical standard. The Spirit *will* guide and transform you, step by step.

So what happens after you honestly discern which things are and which are not options for your free resources (time, money, and energy)? What's the next step?

Loving Obedience

When I think of the next step in discerning how to spend our free time and money, François Fénelon's words (from the eighteenth century!) hit the nail on the head. A shrewd spiritual director, Fénelon straightforwardly exposed our tendency to justify and excuse self-proclaimed "small matters."

In *Talking with God*, Fénelon wrote, "Indeed, it sometimes happens that we find it harder to part with a trifle than with an important interest. It may be more of a cross to us to abandon a vain amusement than to give a large gift to charity. We are more easily deceived about small matters if we imagine them to be innocent and think that we are indifferent to them."[7]

What would the trifles of our day be? A television show or website? A type of book? A "license" for how long to shop or how much to spend after a hard week? What vain amusements would be more difficult for you to give up than it would be to give a large amount to charity?

Fénelon continued, "'It is a small matter,' they say. That is true, but it is of amazing consequence to you. It is something you love enough to refuse to give it up to God. It is something you sneer at in words, so that you may have an excuse to keep it: a small matter—but one that you withhold from your Maker, which can prove your ruin."[8]

We may sneer at our vain amusements with words like, "Oh, that? It's nothing. I could give it up in a heartbeat." But then God asks us to surrender it—maybe not with a voice thundering from heaven but, like

Kara experienced with romance novels, through a continual impression of the heart, through sermons and readings—and we turn a deaf ear to the Spirit's promptings.

Fénelon summed up brilliantly: "The greatest danger of all is this: by neglecting small matters, our soul becomes accustomed to unfaithfulness."[9]

I don't want my soul to become accustomed to unfaithfulness. I don't want to neglect small matters. I need discernment to figure out what God is asking me to surrender. Then I want to lovingly obey.

It's as simple—and *agonizingly difficult*—as that.

Six centuries before Fénelon, Saint Bernard of Clairvaux explained that the human soul always becomes like what it desires. It doesn't take much time to observe that the natural state of a modern person's soul is broken and dispersed. Why? Because we desire too many things, and the things we long for are merely fleeting reflections of what will actually satisfy.

Clairvaux stated, "The immortal soul desiring changeable and perishing things becomes vacillating and fearful of losing what it desires, and its essential freedom is chained by its desires. . . . When we seek things that are below ourselves because of their mutability and corruptibility, we ourselves become unsettled, restless, seeking change, unsatisfied, and unhappy."[10]

We were made for eternity. Our immortal souls were created for perfect love, unity, and harmony. But because we long for the perishable and ephemeral things of the world more than we do the immutable and incorruptible God, we become slaves to (and just like) the things we want: restless, unfulfilled, divided.

The only path to satisfaction is that of *unified desire*, of *undivided heart*. This is why Christ told His beloved ones, "You are worried and distracted by many things; there is need of only one thing" (Luke 10:41-42, NRSV).

We are worried and distracted by so much during our free time. We are distracted by media, overly concerned with having fun, worried about our finances, busy rushing about after the fleeting desires of our hearts, things that can never bring us the life we crave.

There is need of only one thing.

Will you pray with the psalmist and with me?

Tell me where you want me to go, [LORD,] and I will go there. May every fiber of my being unite in reverence to your name. With all my heart I will praise you. I will give glory to your name forever, for you love me so much! You are constantly so kind! You have rescued me from deepest hell. (Psalm 86:11-13, TLB)

May every fiber of our beings unite to fear God, to lovingly obey Him. May no "small matter" separate us from the God who is so constantly kind, who loves us so much, who has rescued *all of us* (no matter how good we think we've been compared to "them") from deepest hell.

Aiming Higher

We've clearly seen that what we do in our free time dramatically affects the state of our souls, the unity or division of our hearts, the purity or corruption of our minds. And as Jerry Bridges commented in *The Pursuit of Holiness*, "If we have not made a commitment to holiness without exception, we are like a soldier going into battle with the aim of not getting hit very much."[11]

I don't want to pursue holiness with exceptions. In the epic battle between heaven and hell—the battle for the purity of my eternal soul—I want to aim higher than "not getting hit very much." What about you?

As we ask the Holy Spirit to help us ruthlessly self-evaluate, act on accurate self-knowledge, lovingly obey God, and then commit to total holiness, we find that the life of set-apartness is far more fulfilling and pleasurable than anything we could devise for ourselves.

With David, let us proclaim of God, "You will teach me how to live a holy life. Being with you will fill me with joy; at your right hand I will find pleasure forever" (Psalm 16:11, NCV).

And let us ask the Holy Spirit to help us actually believe what we proclaim.

Questions for Discussion

1. Have you witnessed Christians (or done so yourself) justifying what they want to do by claiming, "It doesn't affect me" or "It's not that big a deal"? What do you think of this? Do you think my emphasis on honest evaluation and loving obedience is overstated? Why or why not? In what biblical and experiential ways would you support your claim?

2. Author Thomas Merton once claimed, "Even the most sacred realities can be debased and, without totally losing their sacred character, enter into the round of secular 'diversion.'"[12] Do you agree? Is it possible to use Christian activities—worship music, Christian books, even going to church functions—as nothing more than diversion? If so, how do we guard against this in an "entertain me," "life should be fun" world?

3. Is it hard for you to believe that total holiness and purity are pleasurable, that a holy life is actually what you crave? Why or why not? In what ways have life experiences influenced what you believe? How might growing closer to God transform the way you perceive and experience holiness? What do you want to ask God for to help you live out this truth?

Thoughts for Personal Meditation

Take some time to ponder these words from Psalm 101:

> I will refuse to look at
> anything vile and vulgar. . . .
> I will reject perverse ideas
> and stay away from every evil. (verses 3-4, NLT)

Then inventory your free time for one full week. Could anything you looked at (whether reading, watching, or browsing) be considered base, crude, or offensive? Did you specifically choose not to look at something because you recognized it to be vile or vulgar? "Perverse ideas" in verse 4 refers to contrary or rebellious thoughts. What disobedient or crooked thinking tempted you during your free time this week? What commitment would you like to make to God for the weeks ahead?

A Prayer to Spark Your Conversation with God

Lord God, Your revelation pulls my life together and makes it whole. You point me in the right direction again and again. But You do more than that—You show me the way of joy, too. You guard me from danger and lead me to hidden treasure. You are amazing, God! I want to honor You with my every decision. You deserve no less. As I choose how to spend the free time and money that You've given me, may Your guidance be plain and my commitment to holiness complete. May the things I determine to do and the unspoken thoughts that accompany them please You, O Lord, my Rock and my Redeemer. Amen.[13]

SIX

Your Divine Invitation

EXERCISING VOCATIONAL DISCERNMENT

WHILE STUDYING AT RICE University and continuing on the "I will succeed" warpath I described in chapter 1, I chose majors that would launch me into either international law or business. Raging drivenness also propelled me into the Phi Beta Kappa society and an inner void so consuming that any accomplishment was shrouded with this question: Can you keep it up? After graduation, another question descended on me with full force: What in the world is next?

But in the midst of all this, I heard God saying, as if for the first time, *I have something more for you.* And not something more in the sense of one additional thing to put on my agenda, one more activity that would ensure ultimate fulfillment. No, God spoke to my heart of a *more* that would transform my endless grasping for success and achievement into a vibrant call, not to "be all that you can be," but to "be what I've created you to be."

As I'd been years earlier when deciding where to attend college, I was at a crossroads. But this time, hearing God's voice was of utmost importance to me. I knew I couldn't simply make up my mind. Instead, I listened, inclining my heart and choices to the Spirit's calling, a calling deeper and truer than the inner drivenness I'd surrendered to so many times before.

I wanted to give my entire life to God. Naively, I thought that automatically meant I should go into full-time Christian ministry. Since I was single, I (also naively) believed that my options were limited. I could think of nothing other than to submit applications to mission agencies. I know it's laughable, but I actually thought, *What else can single Christian women do for God?*

Transparent and passionate at twenty years old, I felt I should inform these agencies right off the bat what my strengths and weaknesses were. I wrote a very authentic cover letter detailing my battle with the sins of perfectionism and the eating disorder that grew out of it. I mailed my applications and letters to the base-level, "send your information" addresses for several prominent mission organizations.

Not one of them responded. Well, that's not entirely true. The college-ministry arm of one of the agencies sent me an information packet, but I was an early graduate, only twenty years old. I didn't think college students, many of whom might be older than me, would take me seriously.

I was crushed and confused. Though it felt different from when I faced disappointment in my teenage years, this rejection forced me to face some similar questions: What went wrong? Wasn't this the plan? What's to become of me? And this time, since I was *really* trying to do God's will, everything seemed more complicated. I feared that I'd misheard God, that I was in sin, or that He was capriciously pulling the rug out from under me (as zealous as I was for the Lord, I still held many dreadfully false notions about Him).

Needing money, I took a job as a waitress. I worked ten to four thirty every weekday and spent a good deal of my time off trying to figure out God's will for my life. About this time, I met with the senior pastor of our church and his wife. As I communicated my heart and what I felt God was calling me to do, Dale suggested that I check out serving in the youth ministries at our church. He'd listened attentively to my desire to help young people avoid some of the traps of appearance and achievement that I'd so furiously fallen into. Perhaps, he suggested, volunteering with youth would be a good place to start.

I eventually took on the role of mentoring eight sophomore girls. And I absolutely fell in love with them. I eagerly anticipated our weekly Bible study time and felt like a live wire when explaining to them what God had taught and was teaching me every day.

During this time, questions about whether I should or would have a career still loomed large in the background. I also remember feeling, more fiercely than ever before, the desire to be a wife and mother. In fact, at a luncheon for female youth-group volunteers, I candidly confessed that I believed this was a "real calling."

Even though I didn't fully understand the term *calling*, I had noticed that in Christian circles it was generally accepted and used as a way of saying something between "This is what I want to do" and "This is what I think God wants me to do." The trouble was that I currently had no marital prospects.

Little did I know that Jeramy, who was one of the staff members at our church, and I would fall madly in love and marry nine months to the day after our first date (and less than a year from when I made that rather embarrassingly transparent admission to the other youth-group leaders).

In choosing to weave my life together with Jeramy's, I also discovered that the "call" I had sensed two years earlier to go into ministry was real, but it was different than I imagined and definitely not fulfilled on the schedule I anticipated. Jeramy was graduating from seminary and about to take his first full-time job as a youth pastor. So I became—all at once—not only a wife but a pastor's wife.

When Jeramy came home a few months into our marriage and told me he felt called to write a book, I thought he was joking. But he was completely serious and wanted me to do it with him. Again I had to ask, *What are You doing, Lord? What am I to do?* By this time I had become a bit more disciplined in the art of listening for God's guidance. So after prayer and meditation and seeking the counsel of others, Jeramy and I embarked on the adventure of writing a book together.

As I sit here now, writing the seventh book God has brought into my life, I am astounded and amazed at how God has revealed Himself and His callings in my life. But only as I began to research for this particular work could I see these experiences in light of an important, although nearly forgotten, doctrine of the Christian faith—vocation.

Defining Our Terms

I'd venture to guess that many of you tend—like I once did—to view your current life and future in the light of career choices and lifestyle options (say, for instance, marriage versus singleness or being part of a big church versus a small one). You probably *don't* think of your life in terms of vocation.

In fact, the word *vocation* has almost completely fallen out of common parlance. When it is used today, it's usually done so in a way that makes vocation mistakenly synonymous with work. If we're to enter any discussion about vocation, we need to define our terms.

In his illuminating book *God at Work*, Gene Veith offered this helpful and basic information: Vocation is a theological term that reflects a broad spectrum of biblical teaching about work, family, community, and the spiritual life. Our English word *vocation* is derived directly from the Latin term for *calling* (*vocare*).[1]

Vocation carries a wide variety of meanings, each multifaceted and faith laden. A central theme of every definition of vocation, however, is that of *calling*. Through our vocations, God invites us to embrace roles and responsibilities that stretch from the simplest daily tasks to the most profound charges of our lives.

Biblically speaking, vocation connotes two primary things. The first, and by far the most prevalent, is the call to membership and active participation in God's family. We see this meaning reflected in verses such as 1 Corinthians 1:9: "God is faithful; by him you were *called* into the fellowship of his Son, Jesus Christ our Lord" (NRSV, emphasis added).

The second meaning, and the focus of this chapter, concerns personal and particular callings—special tasks and/or positions for which God prepares, and to which God invites, individuals.

In Exodus 31:1-5, while giving instructions for the building of His tabernacle, "GOD spoke to Moses: 'See what I've done; I've personally chosen Bezalel son of Uri, son of Hur of the tribe of Judah. I've filled him with the Spirit of God, giving him skill and know-how and expertise in every kind of craft to create designs and . . . to carve wood.'"

God called Bezalel to the vocation of artistry and craftsmanship. This call was personal (he was chosen by name), purposeful (through his work, Bezalel would help carry out God's plan for the tabernacle), and for which he had been prepared (God gave Bezalel "skill and know-how and expertise").

This, the first biblical reference to a person being "filled . . . with the Spirit of God," displays *both* scriptural forms of vocation. Bezalel was called not only to have an indwelling relationship with his Creator but also to exercise the ability and creativity God gave him for specific purposes.

I find it amazing and inspiring that God "filled [Bezalel] with the Spirit of God" to adorn the tabernacle. How magnificently this reveals God's desire for and appreciation of beauty. How profoundly this challenges the idea that to work for God you must do and be certain things.

Later in Exodus, Moses communicated God's plans to the Israelites and explained that Bezalel and another craftsman, Oholiab, would use their skills not only "to do all kinds of work" (35:35, NCV) but also "to teach others" (35:34, NCV). God's call on Bezalel's and Oholiab's lives included a dimension of communal and social responsibility. They were to train others in the work for which God had equipped them.

The story culminates in Exodus 36:2 when "Moses called Bezalel, Oholiab, and all the other skilled people to whom the LORD had given skills, and they came because they wanted to help with the work" (NCV). Did you catch the last part of that verse? The craftsmen came because they *wanted* to help with the work. In the NRSV, Exodus 36:2 reads, "Every skillful one to whom the LORD had given skill, everyone whose heart was stirred" came to do the work. From this we discern another incredibly important aspect of vocation: God's calls on our lives intersect not only with our Spirit-given abilities and His purposes but with our desires, interests, and passions as well.

Of course, it's essential to recognize that desire wasn't the *only* way people determined if they were called to this particular work. The passage makes it clear that those to whom God had given *both* skill and desire might identify themselves as called to the project. Still, the artists' hearts *were* stirred, and from the descriptions God later gives us of the tabernacle, we know that in responding to their call and embracing their vocations, these men worshipped God by creating breathtaking beauty.

Have you ever felt your heart stirred to do something? Perhaps as a child you longed to be a doctor or astronaut when you grew up. You may not have ended up in med school or at NASA, but I wonder if your desire to help people or explore unknown places was carried out in other ways.

Maybe, however, the yearnings that once stirred your heart have been quieted. Thorns and thistles inevitably threaten us; they can crowd out the good fruit God would bear through our lives and destroy our sense of calling. As *God at Work* reveals, "In not being aware of what their vocations are—and that there is a spiritual dimension to work, family, and involvement in society—[many people] are plagued by a lack of purpose, confused as to what they should do . . . how they should live and who they are."[2]

Viewing our lives through the lens of vocation—and in the multilayered way evidenced through the story of the Old Testament craftsmen—helps all of us who live in a fragmented and complex society integrate the various aspects of our lives: home and office, community and church, even our personal faith.

Let's look at some specific facets of the doctrine of vocation that will help us grow not only in discernment but also in our understanding of the significant role we play in God's creative and ongoing work here on earth.

Serving God Through Serving Others

God calls every person not merely to one vocation but to *multiple* vocations throughout his or her life—at work, in the family, at school, in the greater community, and within God's eternal church.

We experience our first vocations within the family. The roles we play as sons, daughters, sisters, brothers, and eventually, should God ordain it, as fathers, mothers, uncles, aunts, grandparents, and in-laws are truly holy callings.

The multidimensional reality of family life also reveals a significant truth about vocation as a whole: We can hold several vocations within a particular sphere—we may simultaneously be children, parents, grandparents, and siblings. This is likewise true of God's church, in which we are both served and are servants; at work, where we might manage and be supervised; and in the communities we both are governed by and help govern democratically.

In addition, the often difficult dailiness of family life shows that we can view every task, no matter how small, as an expression of the unique call of God on our lives. It also shows that certain vocations call out of us emotional and volitional responses, which we could never create or maintain.

As Jeramy and I vowed to love and serve one another till death do us part, I committed to the vocation of marriage (though back then I couldn't have articulated it in those terms). I also committed myself to the possibility of motherhood, and when I gave birth to our first child, the call on my heart to mother Jocelyn was undeniable and joyful. But the vocations of marriage and parenthood called forth within me—and continue to call forth—a deeper love than I can manufacture or sustain.

In *Luther on Vocation*, theologian Gustaf Wingren explored this amazing dimension of vocation:

> *The human being is self-willed, desiring that whatever happens shall be to his own advantage. [Thus,] when husband and wife, in marriage, serve one another and their children, this is not due to the heart's spontaneous and undisturbed expression of love, every day and hour. Rather, in marriage as an institution something compels the husband's selfish desires to yield and likewise inhibits the ego-centricity of the wife's heart. At work in marriage is a power which compels self-giving to spouse and children.*[3]

In a society where individuals tend no longer to "belong" to a family but rather to "use" a family to meet their own needs, the idea that we are called to serve—and equipped by God to serve—our families (even when our hearts are not spontaneously moved to love) is particularly challenging and inspiring.

And the fact that certain vocations call out of us that which we could never create or maintain also illustrates why it's so important—absolutely *crucial*—that we exercise discernment before pursuing a particular vocation. Vocation is a calling, not merely a choice, and we can't rush in expecting fulfillment from something that is not genuinely our God-given station, even a good thing like marriage or a service career.

Indeed, the modern association between particular vocations and self-fulfillment runs completely counter to biblical tradition. When we make decisions about where to go to college, whether to get married, and what occupation to train for, we usually think in terms of what will make us happy. But vocation is not *fundamentally* about self-actualization.

Now, this doesn't mean God couldn't care less if we experience joy and satisfaction in our callings. On the contrary, as in the case of the tabernacle craftsmen of old, the Spirit will often stir our hearts. God's truth does indicate, however, that our gratification cannot be the only, or even the primary, purpose for pursuing certain positions (even "good Christian" ones).

In addition, though the doctrine of vocation certainly concerns human work, achievement, and fulfillment, on the most important level our callings are about *God's* work in and through our lives. Vocation is, first and foremost, about serving God through serving others.[4]

God designed us to need one another. Americans, including American Christians, place unequaled value on independent self-sufficiency. But our complete dependence on other people becomes obvious when we realize that the clothes we wear were designed, patterned, cut, and sewn by *someone*. The money we "make" was printed and minted by *someone*. The food we prepare was grown and shipped to the grocery store by *someone else*. In a crazy way, it seems easier for people to acknowledge their dependence on God in the spiritual realm than it does their dependence on others in the earthly sphere.

While our relationship to God does not depend on our works, our relationships with other people and with the very earth are interdependent. God does not need our good works, but other people do.[5]

God uses farmers and fast-food workers to provide sustenance. He uses executives and electricians to run our economies and bring us light. He uses actors to entertain and pastors to preach. He uses nurses and nannies, singles and spouses. He works through every calling to accomplish a glorious plan for His beloved children. He has an eternal purpose and many vocations for *you*. He wants you to embrace each of them.

Doing so brings unity to our lives. As we begin to view our paid work, home life, community roles, recreation, and friendships as particular callings in response to the most important and basic call in our lives—to devote everything we are and do to Christ—we find ourselves working with Him to bring life and love to all people. The truth that God is working through and behind our vocations is incredibly liberating. Gene Veith rightly reflected,

> *Above all, vocation is a matter of Gospel, a manifestation of God's action, not our own. In this sense, vocation is not another burden placed upon us, something else to fail at [or figure out], but a realm in which we can experience God's love and grace, both in the blessings we receive from others and in the way God is working through us despite our failures.*[6]

Perhaps you're wondering at this point, *Well, how in the world am I to find what my vocations are? How do I determine God's callings for my life?* Now that we've begun to reorganize—if only in part—our thinking about vocation, let's explore how discernment helps us respond to these important and often bewildering questions.

Chosen, Destined, or Discovered?

Previously I noted that vocation is not simply a choice. Vocation is also not the proverbial needle in a haystack. Our vocations aren't mysteriously buried "out there," waiting for us to discover them.

God doesn't predetermine every detail of our lives in some cosmically inflexible blueprint, in a way that we can miss our calling to marry the "right" person or pick the "right" career. Rather, as Douglas Schuurman observed in *Vocation: Discerning Our Callings in Life*, "God's providence . . . lead[s] us to the humble self-understanding that as finite, limited beings God calls us only to do our part, at this time and in this place."[7] Indeed, some of our vocations are immediately recognizable, right where we are and in what we're presently doing.

You needn't wonder if you're called to love God, to respect your parents, or even to be a student through the twelfth grade. These things are commanded (honoring God and your family members) or compulsory (education through the twelfth grade is typically required, if not enforced, by the state).

If you have a job of any kind, you've been called by God to submit to your supervisors and meet the needs of His people through your work. As a waitress, I helped provide nourishment for people. Working in a restaurant wasn't something I felt particularly called to do. But after taking the job, I could *decide* to enjoy working with God as He accomplished one of His purposes: sustaining people with food.

While we may be preparing for and wanting to do some other future work, that shouldn't distract us from the relationships, responsibilities, and roles that God's given us right now. Perhaps we fail to recognize the vocations we have at the present time because we believe that participating in God's work must look a certain way. But as we can see through the story of Bezalel, serving God and others doesn't automatically mean "church work" or even finding some distinctly "Christian" way of doing work. Believers and nonbelievers perform many of the same tasks. Disciples of Jesus, however, have the blessing of *viewing* their work in an eternal way.

On top of this prevalent but misguided perception that God's callings and work always take a particular form, people sometimes add the assumption that being called is a rare or extraordinary event, in which God "tells" someone to enter a specific career path, get married to a particular person, or significantly change his or her life in some other way.

It's a mistake to assume that God works *only* in, as the oft-used phrase says, "mysterious ways." Truly, He often does. But He also (and perhaps more often) uses ordinary means to accomplish His purposes. Too often we expect our vocational callings to be clearly and distinctly "of Him"—sort of supernatural and "otherworldly."

But we experience our callings most often in ordinary ways and through ordinary means. God didn't hang a neon sign over Jeramy's head that told me, "Marry this one!" As scholar Douglas Schuurman pointed out,

> *God's call is not normally experienced as an audible, miraculous voice or visible sign in the heavens; rather, the lens of faith discerns God's call in and through the duties and opportunities of our varied social locations. . . . For the vast majority of Christians God's callings are discerned quietly, when the heart of faith joins opportunities and gifts with the needs of others. . . . As we open ourselves up to the needs of the world, we gain and regain a sense of calling.*[8]

There's a charming tale related to this idea that Midwesterners sometimes tell: "Once upon a time, a young man saw a vision in the night sky. Upon the starry blanket of the heavens were scrawled the initials P.C. A devout lad, the boy assumed that God was calling him to Preach Christ. In fact, the Lord wanted him to Plant Corn." Though people sometimes want mystical experiences, spectacular revelations, and supernatural work to do, God brings vocation down to earth and allows us to see how close He really is. He wants some people to plant corn.

Martin Luther, the revolutionary theologian, went so far as to say that vocation is a "mask of God." God hides Himself in offices and homes, churches and farms. God isn't far above the mundane details of the ordinary world. Certainly He transcends them and is far greater than any earthly thing. But by drawing near to us in what we do, day in and day out, He transforms the daily grind.

The question remains, however: Will we let Him? Will we let Him show us how normal life can be holy and creative and specifically designed for us?

If we open ourselves to His guidance, if we listen closely and observe attentively, we come to find that though the Bible doesn't provide a formula for discerning God's callings, it does determine key elements of wise, vocational decision making. These include giftings, interests, needs, obligations, mentoring, discussion, and prayer. Frederick Buechner beautifully described the interplay of these basic facets of vocational discernment: "The place God calls you is the place where your deep gladness and the world's deep hunger meet."[9]

Finding your vocations then, has to do in part with identifying your God-given passions (the tabernacle craftsmen's hearts were stirred) and talents (they were also skilled for the work), as well as the needs you might be equipped to meet (God used them to meet the need for artists to adorn His dwelling place).

What so often happens, however, particularly in regard to college or career decisions, is that people pay more attention to what will provide self-fulfillment, financial stability, or both.

Consider Janie and Bridgette, bright girls who read that pharmaceutical reps are currently in high demand and are consequently being paid better than ever. They both take the training courses. Janie flunks;

she recognizes that a career in pharmaceutics isn't for her.

But what about Bridgette, whose math and social skills propel her to the top of her class and land her a great job? Bridgette starts her new career but despises the work; she hates traveling and trying to persuade doctors that they need her products. She doesn't experience her work as a God-given calling.

Bridgette knows that the world needs people to manufacture, market, and sell medicine. These are legitimate needs. Her skill set complements the work, and it certainly isn't wrong of her to want to make enough money for things like food, shelter, and clothing. Still, the deep disappointment Bridgette experiences makes her wonder, *Did I miss out on my opportunity to discern and live in God's particular vocations for me?*

Absolutely not.

Bridgette talks her difficulties over with both her grandmother, a wise and godly woman, and her pastor. She also prays about the situation quite a bit. She doesn't quit her job but faces her disappointment squarely. Why? Because she doesn't sense God immediately calling her out of the vocation that she at present finds little joy in. She certainly could have given her two-weeks notice and taken a job elsewhere.

Instead, Bridgette discerns that the restless discontentment with where she is right now doesn't necessarily mean God is calling her to something new. It may actually indicate the need for renewed prayer and obedience right where she is.[10]

Bridgette continues serving for some time but with a new perspective on her work. Later, she feels released from the position and called to marriage and motherhood. Bridgette now uses her business savvy to run a part-time home business, something she wouldn't have been able to do without the training and experience she was given through the pharmaceutical company.

Through Bridgette's story we see that "our surroundings shake us, sift us, and draw our vocation[s] from us. . . . Mentors also call forth our vocations. They are people with experience who point out our gifts and help us develop them."[11]

We exercise vocational discernment so that we can discover not simply what we will do but also who we are or might be. To determine if we are to preach Christ, plant corn, or parent children, we must exercise discernment. We can evaluate how the gifts God has given us, the needs around us, the desires of our hearts, the counsel of mentors, and the guidance of the Spirit fit together. In doing this, the vocations to which He's called us become more readily evident.

But What About . . .

At this stage, I can almost hear some of your sighs. "That's all well and good," you may say. "You were invited to the vocations of marriage and motherhood and ministry. Those calls were obviously of God. And you're happy. I'm not. I want to be a mother but am twenty-seven and single. I thought I made some good choices about my future, but I'm still miserable and can't see any way out. I don't think I have any special gifts, let alone something that will 'meet the world's deepest hunger,' like that quote said. What am I supposed to do?"

Whether you feel some or all of this, I understand. Truly, I do. I, too, have felt restless discontentment with my stations in life. I've done my share of wondering: *Did I do something wrong? Did I miss God's plan for me? Is this as good as it gets?*

Here's the tragic reality of our broken world: The exalted and beautiful truths about vocation must be held in balance with the fact that we will *all* experience frustration, disappointment, and unmet longings. I just can't say it better than Gene Veith:

From the perspective of the people slaving away in [difficult] vocations, their work is often a daily grind, a hard, boring, thankless task.

Those in any particular line of work are usually doing it not from some high ideal but because they have to make a living. There may be some professions that are innately satisfyingly but even high-paid and high-status jobs can wear the spirit down. Work often appears meaningless. It is a means to an end — survival; but it seems that we survive only to work. It consumes our time, our emotions, our after-hours preoccupations. It takes away the time we would like to spend with our families — though the vocation of family life is often a frustrating struggle as well — and as current technology puts us on call twenty-four hours a day, seven days a week, our work consumes our lives.[12]

Only in the new heaven and earth will there be complete freedom and fulfillment in our work. Until then, every single calling in our lives will bear the scars of sin along with the glory of God's "very good" creation. In his *Treatises*, John Calvin summed things up powerfully: "There is simply no vocation in which a great deal of abuse is not committed."[13]

Economic troubles and fierce competition plague our relationships with other workers. Family members wound us deeply, and bitterness threatens to overwhelm the love to which we are called. Our work within the church is tiring and sometimes seems fruitless. Thankfully, the doctrine of vocation takes into account these hardships, challenges, and failures.

Even though we won't have the perfect answers for every query or be able to make the best decisions at every point, we can find comfort in looking at how our brokenness and the sins of others affect the vocations to which God invites us. In *God at Work*, Gene Veith stressed that every sin is a violation of one's callings, a betrayal of one's vocations.[14] Because the focus of our vocations and the ultimate purposes behind them are to love and serve God and one's neighbors, failing to do so constitutes a transgression against who we are and were created to be. In short, refusing to act within our vocations, or deliberately acting outside of them, is sin.

Viewing marriage as a vocation helps us understand why only husbands and wives are sanctioned with sexual freedom. Since sex is not something single people are invited to do, to engage in sexual acts outside of marriage is a violation of one's calling; it is a sin.

In less extreme examples, we can violate our callings without transgressing moral laws. We may be innocent of specific wrongdoing, but acting outside of our vocation can often result in frustration, ineffectiveness, and wasted time. Let me give you an example. My father is *not* a handyman. When the trash compactor at my parents' house broke, my dad could've squandered hours of his time trying to fix it. Out of some ideal of American self-sufficiency or the misguided notion that an intelligent person should be able to figure out whatever he sets his mind to, my father could've tackled the job. I guarantee he would've created a huge mess, thrown up his hands in despair, and joked (though perhaps with a bit of seriousness) that the thing was possessed. Instead, he wisely wheeled the trash compactor into the workshop. He asked Jeramy to take a look at it, and after ten minutes, Jeramy had it up and running. My dad, amazed and amused, commented, "I'd rather have someone tell me to write a symphony."

My father is a composer (and a brilliant one as far as I'm concerned). One of his vocations is to bring beauty and light into the world through melody and counterpoint. My husband is a pastor (and a phenomenal one, if you ask me). One of his primary vocations is to speak God's truth to people and lead them in our church. But another of Jeramy's vocations seems to be helping people figure out and fix things. He blesses our family and others with his skill, know-how, and precision. This is *not* one of my dad's vocations. If Jeramy tried to conduct the L.A. Philharmonic, or if my dad attempted to repair the ice maker on his refrigerator, they certainly wouldn't be engaging in any evident immorality. But they would be violating one of their callings by spending time doing that for which they were neither equipped nor excited.

The reality is that we sometimes experience the brokenness of vocation because we act out of what we *assume* we're called to do (whether because we don't want to admit that we can't do everything or because we're genuinely mistaken about what we're supposed to do) rather than what we *really are* invited by God to do.

Temptation also plays a significant role in vocational difficulties. We may be tempted to pride in our position, to laziness, or to despair. All of these can undermine our capacity to work for and with God. "Temptation in vocation," wrote Gustaf Wingren, "is the devil's attempt to get man out of his vocation."[15] He explained that because God calls us to our vocations, the Devil will endlessly endeavor to make us doubtful, discouraged, and ready to quit.

In our weakness and in a world laced at every point with sin and shame, we can cling to the words of 1 Corinthians 15:58, which proclaim, "Stand your ground. And don't hold back. Throw yourselves into the work of the Master, confident that nothing you do for him is a waste of time or effort." Vocational discernment helps us know when to stand our ground and resist temptations, how to work only within our own vocations, and how to see that *nothing* we do for God is a waste of time or effort. Discernment also helps us identify and work against two aspects of vocational temptation that threaten us, often in insidious and undetectable ways—busyness and success.

Restless Volition and Unquenchable Hunger

Most of us are chronically busy and frazzled. Many of us are anxious about the future, not to mention the past and present. We're too frantic and consumed with our daily tasks to feel the current of living water rushing around us, wooing us to work that is eternal and significant.

We no longer value, let alone take a day of, rest. Tragically, some view the Sabbath as an Old Testament requirement that has little to do with our modern life, or, worse, they think that because the Pharisees observed it, it must therefore be part of their legalist tradition. In *The Inner Experience*, however, Thomas Merton negated these ideas: "[We] stop working and rushing about on Sunday not only in order to rest up and start over again on Monday, but in order to collect our wits and realize the relative meaninglessness of the secular business which fills the other six days of the week."[16]

God also shows us that by His power at work in us, *He* can accomplish in six days what we assume will take seven to do. Through the Sabbath, God reminds us that "*in him* we live and move and have our being" (Acts 17:28, NRSV, emphasis added). He is in charge; we are not. We often miss His call to cease striving and know (again, the Hebrew word for this connotes a deep, personal, and experiential knowledge) that *He is God*.

Jesus once declared, "The Sabbath was made to serve us; we weren't made to serve the Sabbath" (Mark 2:27). That is to say, the Sabbath is *God's gift* to us weary humans. In a unique way, through the Sabbath rest, we can taste the satisfaction of a peace that surpasses understanding and that is given to us by Christ. He lovingly offers us a break—an opportunity to spend time with Him, with our families, and by ourselves.

I wonder if one of the reasons God commanded us to keep the Sabbath holy was because He knew we'd constantly be tempted to busyness. We rush about for many reasons, but here are two of the most common: We're afraid to disappoint God and terrified of disappointing everyone else (including ourselves).

Spanish mystic Saint John of the Cross urged us,

> *Let those that are great actives and think to girdle the world with their outward works take note that they would bring far more profit to the*

Church and be far more pleasing to God if they spent even half this time in abiding with God in prayer. Of a surety they would accomplish more with one piece of work than they now do with a thousand and that with far less labour.[17]

We think that our packed-out schedules maximize our time and potential. But if we step back for just a moment, we can readily observe that chronic busyness more often leads to shallow achievements, broken relationships, and estrangement from God.

Even more tragically, frenetic activity indicates that we believe, deep in our heart of hearts, that we're only as good as what we do. Dallas Willard described this as a harassing, hovering sense of "ought to/should/have to/must," which arises principally from the void in our souls, where we should be at peace with God and ourselves.[18]

We cannot experience freedom and fulfillment in our vocations while frantically trying to prove our worth through busy accomplishment. The only cures for this vacuum within are silence and solitude, which break the pell-mell pace and open an inner space that allows us to hear God. In silence and solitude we discover—with complete confidence—that we are more than what we do.

But it requires great discernment to determine when to be active and when to slow down. We cannot eliminate all noise or activity from our lives, but we can make decisions that foster centeredness. We can prioritize and order our schedules. We simply cannot

work to feed our appetites;
Meanwhile [letting] our souls go hungry. (Ecclesiastes 6:7)

We cannot allow our drive for success to determine our vocations.

Some people think worldly success indicates special favor from God. But I agree with the evocative philosopher Martin Buber, who once wrote, "The fact that God is identified with success is *the greatest obstacle* to a steadfast religious life."[19] Indeed, "success is not one of the names of God."[20]

There's certainly nothing wrong with making money. Some people seem called by God to have wealth and use it according to His eternal purposes. But an *insatiable drive* for success typically arises not from our love of God but out of the prideful assumptions that the world owes us something, that life should be comfortable, that we can do anything we set our minds to, and that if we work hard enough, we'll be successful.

In God's economy, however, position, power, and success mean little. As *The Voice of Jesus* author Gordon T. Smith pointed out,

> *What matters most is humility, the willingness to accept who we are . . . [and] the grace to take responsibility for our strengths and abilities, to live with contentment within the skin that God has given us rather than aspire to be someone other than who we are. . . . Part of accepting our world and seeing our circumstances in truth is accepting the opportunities that are given to us rather than bemoaning what is not there. Indeed it is not so much a matter of accepting as of actually embracing what we have the opportunity to do.*[21]

We aren't all given the gifts and chances to be successful as the world defines it. But if we can discern with humility the unique path God has laid out before us and the dignity that He bestows on *every* vocation, we will experience eternal success, *His* success.

When faced with a vocational decision, Ignatian scholar Stefan Kiechle counseled us not to ask, "Which of these options will further my monetary success or personal fulfillment?" but rather, "Which of the two [or more] alternatives—given my talents and my limitations—will provide me with an opportunity to contribute more to efforts of making the world a bit more just, peaceful, filled with love, merciful, faithful, and hopeful?"[22]

Furthermore, which option will lead us toward God and away from the lusts of the flesh, the envy of those who appear more successful than we are? When we jealously covet the possessions or positions of others, we find ourselves doubly blinded. We become, all at once, blind to the difficulties that would inherently accompany the vocation we envy and to the opportunities for growth and service in our current situation.[23]

Both busyness and success can undermine the good work that God gives us within our vocations. Both limit our vision and shrink our faith. We must carefully discern how to use our time and pursue our goals, keeping in mind the truths about vocation that continually transform our thinking.

In Summary

Clearly, the Christian life is lived in and through vocation, in the everyday and ordinary tasks of life that consume most of our time and energy. Such things may have appeared mundane before, but as we've seen, God is present in every aspect of our work—at home or church, in the marketplace and greater society. He calls each of us to these spheres, using us in powerful, although often masked, ways.

The doctrine of vocation confers dignity on *you* and the particular callings of *your* life, demonstrating the value and importance of *your* unique talents and inclinations. Vocation also takes into consideration the brokenness of our world. While we'd all love to live in a world where everyone saw his or her work as a way to serve God and others, we know this isn't so. The clerk taking my dry cleaning probably doesn't love me, and if I'm honest, most of the time I'm too busy or distracted to care for her.

But we can choose differently. We can exercise discernment, viewing our callings in life—both the ones obvious here and now, as well as the ones that may come in the future—as God-given opportunities.

The Greek terms *kaleo* and *klesis*, translated as *calling*, can mean either "to summon"/"a summons" or "to invite"/"an invitation." That is why I've deliberately and repeatedly spoken of God inviting us to certain positions and relationships. While a summons carries imperative force, an invitation indicates that we can choose to either respond to or reject God's call.

You don't have to wait to discover your vocations until you graduate or until you have a ring on your left hand. God extends the invitation to us every day. You and I can start today to embrace and enjoy the callings that God has placed on our lives.

Will you accept His adventurous invitations?

Questions for Discussion

MORE (212) 541-6300
INFO (718) 290-2000
CALL (718) 297-7475

1. When William Diehl surveyed Americans and asked whether they experienced a sense of calling in their paid work, 73 percent of those who said yes also reported that they regularly read the Bible.[24] What relationship do you see between these two things? What connection between God's truth and your vocational satisfaction do you experience or hope for?

2. Consider these words, found in Saint John of the Cross's spiritual classic *Dark Night of the Soul*:

> *Those who long to do Thee pleasure and to give Thee something at their cost, setting their own interests last, are very few. The failure, my God, is not in Thy unwillingness to grant us new favours, but in our neglect to use those that we have received in Thy service alone, in order to constrain Thee to grant them to us continually.*[25]

What vocational gifts might you have neglected because they cost you something?

3. How do envy and competition for success—for the rewards of being, say, a better parent than someone else or the best real estate agent in the region—keep us from serving and delighting in other people? Apply this to a recent circumstance in your own life or in the life of someone close to you.

Thoughts for Personal Meditation

Read Acts 9:1-31. Before his encounter with Jesus Christ on the road to Damascus, Saul displayed a keen mind (his comprehensive grasp of the Hebrew Bible and Jewish tradition were unparalleled) and inflamed passion (his zeal for persecuting the followers of the Way was also beyond comparison). Notice how after his conversion, Paul's new callings never changed these aspects of his personality and training. Instead, his new vocations redirected and transformed them.[26] How might God desire to redirect and transform skills or passions that you haven't used for Him? Take some time to explore how your vocations have changed, are changing, and might change in the future. Commit to what God's shown you with thankful prayer, repentance, and/or supplication.

A Prayer to Spark Your Conversation with God

O God, give me the grace to be faithful in my actions, but indifferent to success. It is up to You to crown my feeble actions with such fruit as is pleasing to You—and none at all, if that is what You find best for me. May Your name be hallowed in my works, keeping me in remembrance that You are the doer of all that is really done: my part is that of a humble collaborator, giving of my best.[27]

SEVEN

Relationships Are Messy

DISCERNMENT IS NECESSARY

MY GIRLFRIEND PAIGE WORKS with the poorest of the poor, the kind of people most of us ignore. She loves others with an infectious intensity that makes me want to join her, to change the world at her side. But Paige admits that she is far from perfect in relating to people. In a recent e-mail, she responded to some questions I asked about how discernment helps her in her most challenging relationships. Here's what she wrote:

> As long as I can remember, I've struggled with being judgmental. As an adolescent I "had it together" spiritually (or so I thought). If someone gave me the rules, I followed them to a tee. Now I realize that living with this kind of teeth-gritted, "I will be holy" determination had less to do with God and His people than it did me and my goals. Whatever it took, I was going to do things right. I expected the same focus out of every other believer, especially my "picture-perfect" family.

I wish I could have seen back then that pride made up a big part of the "love" I had for my parents and brother. People saw my family as the ones who were walking with God, the ones making an impact for eternity. And I loved it.

But then I got the call from Mom about my twin brother, Eric, and that was the beginning of a journey that forced me to evaluate how I relate to others. Over the past three years, God has revealed and continues to reveal how pain and confusion in my relationships challenge my ability to make good decisions. I want to make choices that will mold me into the image of Christ and make me a messenger of His unfailing love. In daily relationships with other people, however, this can become incredibly complicated.

The news about Eric I got three years ago winded me like a kick in the gut. I sobbed for hours at the "stupidity of his choices" (I know that sounds harsh). As far as I was concerned, he chose to ruin his life. The summer before, I'd been so relieved when Eric and his non-Christian girlfriend, Charlotte, broke up; I'd even prayed to that end. But then they totally blew it; they got pregnant. At the time, I could barely say that word. Why didn't he follow the rules and stick to the boundaries that both of us had promised to keep? How could he do this to us?

More than for Eric's and Charlotte's spiritual state, I grieved for myself and my family and the loss of our perfect image (isn't that selfish?). I grieved that Eric decided to marry Charlotte and have the baby, rather than give him up for adoption (as I thought all "good Christians" who fell into the trap of passion should do). I grieved for what should have been.

At their wedding I tried so hard to be joyful. But inside I felt sad for them and for me. It wasn't supposed to happen this way. Eric was headed to seminary before he met Charlotte. How could he fall for a nonbeliever?

For months after they became man and wife, I wrestled long and hard, fully aware that the judgmental attitude of my heart kept me from being like Jesus to Eric and Charlotte, but unwilling to let things go. God slowly showed me that I was choosing to act like the Pharisees, gripping their stones to throw at sinners.

He also revealed that my friendship could become a safe place instead, a place where anyone—especially Eric and Charlotte—could feel totally loved, a haven from the storm. Jesus began to draw me out and urged me to follow Him into the depths of love. I hardly imagined that He'd do so by allowing another storm to rage through my life.

Shortly after Charlotte delivered their baby, I discovered that my father—my "perfect" daddy—had betrayed my mother repeatedly, hiding his sin for years. How painful and humbling it was to watch my family crumble. I ached inside, forced to acknowledge that even if a wife does everything "by the Book," as I perceived my mom did, there are no guarantees her husband will make wise choices.

But what's crazy is that it's been easier for me to forgive my adulterous dad than my brother and Charlotte, who other people view as "such a nice couple." For Dad, God seemed to infuse me with forgiveness and renewed respect miraculously, even though by most anyone's standards, he didn't deserve either.

I'm not entirely sure why it's been so difficult for me to forgive and love my brother and his wife. I think part of it is that even though we're twins, Eric always looked to me in spiritual matters. I wondered if I could've or should've done something to stop him. Intellectually, I knew I wasn't responsible, but I often felt guilty and ashamed. Conflicted emotions like these kept me from authentically seeing Eric and Charlotte's condition.

But as God has plowed up the soil of my heart, He's allowed me to discern where Eric and Charlotte really are spiritually. For a long time, I didn't want to see how far my brother had chosen to walk away from the Lord. I wanted to cling to the illusion that Eric was a strong Christian who'd made a mistake or two and that Charlotte was on her way to knowing Christ. But through unrealistic optimism, I'd kept the real Eric and Charlotte at a distance.

God wouldn't let me hide from the truth any longer. He wanted me to get close; He asked me to know and love Eric and Charlotte just as they are. Since we lived on opposite ends of the country, what that meant for me was deciding to send e-mails and make phone calls (even when neither Eric nor Charlotte responded), giving gifts, and praying, praying, praying for freedom from judgment. It also meant trying to understand them as best I could, asking questions about what they thought and enjoyed, what was important to them and why. In all of this, I begged the Spirit to help me. He did so by reminding me of a story.

In Luke 7:36-50, you can read the details of what happened when Jesus dined at the home of Simon, a Pharisee. Here's the short version: In the middle of dinner, a broken woman burst on the scene, lavishly loved her Lord, and completely disregarded the judgmental scorn of Simon and his guests. I began to pray that I'd be like this humble woman, who wiped Jesus' feet with her tears, who loved much because her many sins had been forgiven. I didn't want to have Simon's hard, unmerciful heart. I longed to become more and more a vessel of God's grace — to deeply appreciate it and administer it to others.

Though I never would've signed up for all that's gone down in the last three years, I now see that through these challenges in some of my closest relationships, I've grown in ways that I couldn't have otherwise.

I've had to make decisions, many of them putting to death what comes naturally and is ingrained in me to do. I only hope that by *hearing a portion of my story, some of you can discern which choices might help you honor God in and through difficult relationships.*

Echoing Paul's Words

In a day and age when, with a battle cry for authenticity, the world claims that you should be 100 percent true to your feelings and steer clear of people who wound you, annoy you, or are different from you (despite everyone's talk about tolerance), Christians are continually challenged with how to view and conduct painful relationships.

It's not enough to simply say, "Jesus commands us to love everyone." While this is certainly true and while it is *incredibly* important to remember, God teaches us about another essential component of love, one that transforms simplistic platitudes like "Love the sinner; hate the sin" and "What would Jesus do?" We need bold and life-giving truths that we can actually *live out*, not just nice sayings that fit on bracelets or make us feel better about how we plan to treat others. We need discernment to relate well and help others relate well too.

Taking Paige's story as a case study, we can clearly see that challenges in our relationships require great discernment. Throughout our lives God calls each of us to exercise discernment in forgiving others, seeing people accurately, and learning to love them as they truly are.

Your circumstances may be less dramatic than Paige's or much more painful. The degree of your woundedness and the intensity of your situation—past, present, or future—may stretch you beyond what you think you can handle. On the other hand, you may wonder what the big deal is; you've been able to sail through friendships virtually unscathed. When it comes to discernment, however, it matters little where a person lands on this continuum. We *all* make decisions every day that shape not only us but the people we relate to as well. So this truly is my prayer for you:

That your love will flourish and that you will not only love much but well. Learn to love appropriately. You need to use your head and test your feelings so that your love is sincere and intelligent, not sentimental gush. Live a lover's life, circumspect and exemplary, a life Jesus will be proud of: bountiful in fruits from the soul, making Jesus Christ attractive to all, getting everyone involved in the glory and praise of God. (Philippians 1:9-11)

Wouldn't you like to love much and love *well*? Don't you want to know how to live a "lover's life," a life that makes "Jesus Christ attractive to all"?

How do you respond to the directive that to love appropriately you "need to use your head and test your feelings"? Do the words *sincere* and *intelligent* fit with your ideal picture of love?

I long to love well. I yearn to be loved well too. I desperately want to know how I can make Jesus attractive to all, especially my friends and family who misunderstand (sometimes willfully, I'm sure) who He truly is.

It also seems right and good for me to love sincerely and intelligently, but that honestly sounds a little boring, maybe even forced (we certainly don't find the words, "I love you so intelligently" in our favorite movies or books). Why is it that I often consider spontaneous and passionate love more authentic and desirable than love of a deliberate and chosen kind?

Questions like these challenge us to look at the way we think about relationships. And because within these pages we cannot plumb the depths of all it means to love others well, I'd simply like to explore one aspect of the journey with you: How can discernment help us handle painful and problematic relationships?

Where It All Begins

Before we discuss anything else, and for two very important reasons, we must explore how discernment and forgiveness intersect with our relationships.

First, all of us have been hurt. We all have changed the way we interact with others as a result. And unhealed injuries tend to take root deep within the soul, interfering with our attempts to make any decision, let alone a good one.[1]

Second, while it's true that we've all been wounded, we are also *wounders*. Every person has, in the penetrating words of Evelyn Underhill, "inflicted mental, emotional, and spiritual injury and added to the confusion and pain of the world." Each of us has "abused the sacred gift of freedom, and because of this things are worse than they were before."[2]

This second truth is, perhaps, the more difficult to acknowledge. We may readily admit that we are sinners, but more often than not we mean this in a kind of general, "Oh, we're all human" sort of way. People very rarely face the reality that their decisions have added to humanity's heartache and distress. Are things really worse off because of something, or even some things, *we* have done?

Truly, tragically, yes.

In life, we wound and are wounded. There's simply no way around it. We may try to excuse our "little sins" by comparing them to the "wicked" deeds of others (terrorists, serial killers, or the proverbial "them"), but we also squirm rather uncomfortably when confronted with this reality: Sin is sin.

None of us deserve to be forgiven, and none of us deserve to withhold forgiveness from others either. Discernment—solid thinking and clear vision—helps us own this truth. In *What's So Amazing About Grace?*, Philip Yancey wrote, "In the realm of grace, the word *deserve* does not even apply. . . . Forgiveness breaks the cycle of blame and loosens the stranglehold of guilt . . . through a remarkable linkage, placing the forgiver on the same side as the party who did the wrong. Through it we realize we are not as different from the wrongdoer as we would like to think."[3]

"We are not as different from the wrongdoer as we would like to think." These are difficult words to accept. As often as I have meditated on the truths of forgiveness, even written about them and celebrated their grace, the reality that I am not much different from the people who have hurt me (or traumatized those I love) rattles me to the core.

Like Paige, most of the time I want the higher ground. I want to be able to look down and grant forgiveness from on high, safely shielded from the ugliness of my own sin and shame. God doesn't offer this option.

To love well, we must *choose* to forgive and be forgiven. Discernment helps us completely reorganize our thinking about forgiveness, overhauling lies such as, "Some people don't deserve to be forgiven," "I can forgive others, but I'll never forgive myself," or "Forgiveness is too hard."

As Paige's story so clearly revealed, "forgiving others is not a burden. *Judging others is the burden*, and Jesus begs us to drop it, and take up his burden instead, which is the sweet and light one of forgiving and being forgiven."[4] The sweet and light burden of forgiveness sounds a little paradoxical to me. But these words strike me as paradoxical in the same mysterious way that redemptive suffering and the glory of the Cross do. They are truths that resonate with my heart and mind on a deep level, but a level to which I don't easily descend (or, more appropriately, *ascend*).

In the New Testament, the Greek word most commonly used for forgiveness literally means to let go, to cast aside, to free yourself.[5] To free yourself—isn't that amazing? Through the miraculous grace of God, *you* are freed from both the burden of judging others and the lifelong agony that bitterness brings upon you and others. Forgiveness first and most powerfully transforms the person who forgives.

And still, though the burden of judging others is heavier, forgiveness is not like the simple passing of a sponge over a dirty surface. Instead, Evelyn Underhill described forgiveness as a "stern and painful" process. It requires nothing less than the reordering of the soul's disordered loves. Forgiveness ultimately sets right what is wrong, washes the heart of wickedness, and cleanses it from sin. But it burns to heal, all at once redeeming, transforming, and purifying. Indeed, the refining pain of forgiveness is part of the precious mercy of God.[6]

Being reordered, set right, washed from wickedness, and burned to heal—I know these things are for my good, but if I'm honest, I'm a bit afraid of them too. I can choose forgiveness only by rightly discerning these truths: Hard-heartedness and resentment forge the gates of hell, while generous grace lines the streets of gold; it's my choice to fester or forgive.

Here, at the core of how we view our relationships with God, ourselves, and others lies the intersection of discernment and forgiveness. Here also lie the practical application of grace and the place where phrases like "intelligent love" make perfect sense. We simply cannot forgive the deepest wounds inflicted on us or those we love impulsively or spontaneously. We must *choose*, and choose wisely at that.

Without discerning forgiveness, relationships suffer mortal wounds. Dr. Dan Allender, Christian psychologist and coauthor of *Bold Love*, brought this into sharp focus:

> We will see the importance of forgiveness as a central category in relating to others to the extent that we see every relationship enmeshed in a war that leads to a taste of heaven or hell. . . . Unfortunately, the metaphor of war seems like a television cliché that has lost its punch because most lives are utterly disconnected from the carnage

of a true war . . . but he [the Enemy] works through the dynamics of one person relating to another, attempting to accomplish his destructive goals. The terrain of the eternal war is the battleground of relationships.[7]

Every choice we make, whether a single and enormous one—such as how to forgive a spouse or parent who betrays us—or a repeated and seemingly less-significant one—do we need to forgive the friend who "inadvertently" hurts us again and again?—leads to a taste of heaven or hell for us and for the people with whom we relate.

But the Enemy so cleverly and insidiously disguises the eternal war in which we are engaged behind what Allender called the "humdrum monotony and imperceptible abuses of daily living . . . [so] that a call to arms is ignored as silly adventuring or the paranoid delusions of negativism."[8] In order to grab hold of the life we crave, the truth of our condition must be acknowledged. Our relationships are fraught with the wounds and winds of *war*. If we cannot discern this, we will neither love much nor love well.

Christ calls us to offer others the sincere, intelligent, and discerning love He died to give. Forgiveness does this by inviting the offender to reconciliation with God and with the offended. But this is neither a cheap, blind, "forgive and forget" nor the automatic granting of renewed fellowship.

Forgiveness releases the wounder and wounded, but it does *not* force them together again. If we can borrow some terminology from gaming, forgiveness erases the bet but lends no additional monies until repentance occurs.[9] Through forgiveness, the possibility for new life and new relationships is opened up, but it is never forced. Grace is a gift of free will, not obligation.

Because determining whether or not to reengage with a person who has hurt us is an individual, situational decision, we need to carefully consider the attitude of the offender. God never turns away a genuinely penitent heart, and we can choose to reflect His love in this way.

Of course, this challenges our natural propensities to self-defense and revenge. But forgiveness extended without a genuine desire to see the offender restored to God and others is antiseptic, mechanical, and often more harmful than helpful. As we discern the truth that deep and lasting forgiveness is not only what's good but also the light burden *we crave*, the tide of self-protection can be redirected.

As we end this brief discussion of discernment and forgiveness, I realize the extreme limitations on its depth and breadth. If the ideas in this section have touched a part of you that cries out for more exploration, I urge you to delve into the questions you have. I've included suggestions for discussion and prayer at the end of this chapter. You can also refer to any of the excellent resources from which I've quoted for more help.

But for now, let's transition into a second facet of problematic relationships that calls for discernment—what I call "honest evaluation."

Loving an Illusion

Paige told us she found it more difficult to authentically love her fallen-away twin brother and his non-Christian wife than to forgive her father for years of adultery. She confessed to keeping the real Eric and Charlotte at a distance, loving them only as she thought they should be.

Have you ever found yourself in a similar situation? Have you wanted to withdraw from or gloss over relationships with people who make you uncomfortable, people who just plain bug you, or people who make different decisions than you do (especially if you consider their choices immoral)? I certainly have. I've waffled and wavered and pulled back and then tried to push in again. Sometimes I've sensed God calling me to love people just as they are, but that is a lot easier said than done.

In his masterful book *A Long Obedience in the Same Direction*, Eugene Peterson highlighted a sad hindrance to our loving others much and well. He wrote, "It is far easier to deal with people as problems to be solved than to have anything to do with them in community."[10] Truly, it is much simpler and less demanding to view the Erics and Charlottes in my life as problems that need to be solved—all I have to do is get him to repent and her to accept Christ, and then everything would be fine. What kind of self-righteous attitude would cause me to think in such terms?

I know I'm not the only one, however, who sometimes would prefer to love an illusion or even a "problem" rather than a real person. But how do we reconcile this with the truth: that to love people means seeing them as God intended them to be *and* honestly acknowledging where they are right now?[11]

Real relationships with real people are messy and complicated and always stained with the tragic remains of the Fall. And in the midst of this chaos, God reveals what missionary Frank Laubach called "the simple program of Christ for winning the whole world . . . to make each person he touches magnetic enough with love to draw others."[12] Though it often seems crazy to me, God has chosen to reveal Himself to the world through me and you and every man and woman who chooses to reflect His image. It seems crazy because I know how poorly I sometimes mirror His beautiful and perfect face to the world. But I earnestly crave a life so magnetized by love that it draws others.

Jesuit scholar Gerald O'Mahoney described this life in his book *Abba! Father!* According to O'Mahoney, "You and I, followers of Christ, are invited to look at God and then to become God for our generation." To those around us, we can proclaim, "'My brothers and sisters, you say you cannot see God. Look at me, if you wish to know what God is like.' Such a claim sounds blasphemous at first, but is not that what the disciples of Jesus are supposed to be and to do and to say?" The simple truth is that "we cannot escape 'the incarnation' because there is no one who does not 'make flesh' the god he worships."[13]

Unavoidable questions arise from such bold and thought-provoking statements: "What god do I 'make flesh' as I relate to others?" and "Will I ever be able to say with confidence, 'Look at me, if you wish to know what God is like'?"

As a former perfectionist (now in God's recovery plan of grace), I can assure you that a Christian doesn't have to be sinless to reflect God's image to a wounded world. I'm continually amazed at how God chooses to use me—broken, little, insignificant yet utterly beloved and empowered-with-the-Spirit me—to reveal Himself to others. And He uses me, not in spite of my weaknesses, but *because* of them. My brokenness and inability puts His grace on full and glorious display. Through 2 Corinthians 12:9-10, verses that radicalized my formerly perfectionist life, God has repeatedly affirmed to me, "'My grace is enough for you. When you are weak, my power is made perfect in you.' So I am very happy to brag about my weaknesses. Then Christ's power can live in me. For this reason . . . when I am weak, then I am truly strong" (NCV).

I can't love or relate to people perfectly. But I *can* decide to be a testimony to grace. As pastor and teacher Gordon MacDonald so incisively observed, "The world can do almost anything as well as or better than the church. You need not be a Christian to build houses, to feed the hungry or heal the sick. There is only one thing the world cannot do. It cannot offer grace."[14]

The world can accept people who are different. But it can't extend them grace. The world can encourage people to improve themselves and their situations, but it can't offer them grace. The world can gloss over who and where people really are, but it can't authentically acknowledge their spiritual condition. Grace can.

This is what makes discernment and honest evaluation so incredibly important. The world perceives love as an unconditional acceptance that ignores the bad things you do and practices "random acts of kindness" (which, by the way, are supposed to magically transform everyone into better people). But this is not genuine, Christlike love. As Dallas Willard so wisely and shrewdly observed, for

> most people, to love someone now means to be prepared to approve of their desires and decisions and to help them fulfill them. . . . [But in] the biblical (and any sane) view, to love people means to favor what is good for them and to be prepared to help them toward that, even if that means disapproving of their desires and decisions and attempting, as appropriate, to prevent their fulfillment.[15]

We need discernment to separate people from what they do, to determine what favoring their good and helping them toward that really looks like, even if it means disapproving of their choices and actions, sometimes to the extent that we prevent the realization of desires that would destroy them.

This flies in the face of modern assumptions like, "What people do is strictly their business." Seizing the question Cain asked as his brother's blood cried out from the earth — "Am I my brother's keeper?" (Genesis 4:9, NRSV) — and turning it into a positive imperative, some people declare (often very politely and politically correctly but usually quite forcefully), "Good people mind their own business and don't judge what I do (which is, after all, who I am)."

Even within the church, people (our family, friends, and pastors included) rarely ask about our behavior. We've learned *not* to be our brothers' keepers because the costs seem too great — not only do we risk rejection or condemnation, but we know that engaging with others in this way requires a great deal of us.

And it does. But when we use this as an excuse to shrink back from difficult relationships, whether with Christians or people of different faiths, we miss the fact that we've been given the great privilege and great responsibility of incarnating Christ to people. Discernment helps us grab hold of this, our charge.

Dr. Allender rightly noted that every act of

> *love is a unique blend of invitation and warning — a pull toward life and push away from death. . . . Our love ought to draw others to a taste of life that satisfies like no other, and our strength ought to warn others that pursuit of a false god leads to an abyss that will eventually violate and destroy their soul.*[16]

But to engage with people in this way requires discerning humility, creativity, and courage. We need brave humility because to love those who live in ways that frighten, disgust, or infuriate us forces us to squarely face the depth of our own sin; creativity because only with the redemptive and imaginative application of wisdom can we honestly evaluate where a person is; and a combination of these virtues to sustain our vision for where the people we love might be.

Let me give you an example because we've been digesting some deep truths that might remain obscure or seem impossible unless we flesh them out within the context of real-life circumstances. Two of the most challenging relationships in my life are with women I deeply love but who have made dramatically different choices from me in regard to their faith and sexuality. As a heterosexual, conventionally married Christian, I have struggled to assess Karen and Patty's decisions with humility, compassion, and sober judgment.

I'll be honest: I have no desire to enter into the fiercely debated questions that bristle around the issues of homosexuality and other alternative lifestyles. But I also believe that Christians can no longer ignore the fact that many of us are in relationship — at school, at work, or in our families — with people whose decisions diverge from ours in these sometimes confusing, sometimes maddening ways.

In trying to relate to Karen and Patty as Christ would, I've continually been confronted with the need for discernment. One of the ways I've discerned what is good and loving in my relationships is by trying to see Karen and Patty's choices in the simplest and least dramatic light possible.

To authentically love my friends, I believe I've been called to set aside labels that would identify them purely with the choices they've made. For most of us, categorizing (and/or pigeonholing) helps to mitigate the painful complexity of life. But it also keeps us from compassionately incarnating Christ to the people He's brought into our lives.

I appreciate the way Lewis Smedes described compassion in his insightful work *Sex for Christians*. He wrote, "Compassion is an experience of suffering with someone else's condition. It is neither pity nor moral softness. . . . Compassion gives us an insight into the unique situation and individual character of people who do something that moral principle tells us is improper."[17]

Compassion certainly doesn't lessen the impact or the importance of moral law. Without my strong moral principles, my relationships with Karen and Patty could easily lapse into sentimental tolerance. But devoid of compassion, moralism can disintegrate love, leaving me with impersonal judgmentalism. Discernment helps me remain simultaneously true to the convictions of Scripture and tender to individuals.

Just as Paige recognized that to love Eric and Charlotte required her to enter their world, I've seen that even when I can't identify with Karen and Patty (or the communities in which they live), being present in their lives can be an essential ministry.

The words of Thomas Merton both challenge and inspire me. He counseled,

Do not argue with people, try to convince them, try to convert them, try to make them amend their lives. . . . Seek only to be with them, to share their lives, their poverty, their sufferings, their problems, their ideals: but to be with them in a special way. As members of Christ . . . where [we] are present, Christ is present. Where He is present, He acts. [Our] being, [our] presence is then active, dynamic.[18]

Discernment helps us to creatively stay with our Karens and Pattys in understanding and love, even as they reject what we view as the impartial and absolute guidance of moral law.[19] Discernment gives us the tender, merciful vision to look past sin to the human heart, the heart designed by God for more.

Unfortunately Christians—myself included—haven't always treated people like Karen or Patty with mercy, nor have we continually communicated moral and spiritual truth with grace. But our treating a promiscuous, homosexual, drug-addicted, or any other "easy-to-label" person as a stereotype strips him or her of the personal dignity that God values and longs to redeem. Discernment helps us fight against this.

Discernment also helps us live out Jesus' command in Matthew 10:16: "Stay alert. This is hazardous work I'm assigning you. You're going to be like sheep running through a wolf pack, so don't call attention to yourselves. Be as cunning as a snake, inoffensive as a dove." Dallas Willard illuminated this verse for me in his brilliant work *The Divine Conspiracy*. What are we to learn, Willard asked, from the "wisdom of snakes" and the "innocence of doves"? The snake, he explained, is sharp-eyed and vigilant, displaying wisdom in *timeliness*. When the snake acts, it does so quickly and with certainty. As for the dove, it is free of intrigue. It neither contrives nor guiles. "There is nothing indirect about this gentle creature."[20]

One of my roles in Karen's and Patty's lives is to love without manipulation, to extend grace without contriving. Another role includes patiently watching and waiting for the right opportunity to act, developing in times of waiting the capacity and courage to move decisively when the Spirit does lead me.

I can love without manipulation by learning to genuinely listen (which, in my case, often means listening without an agenda for how I can twist the conversation in a specific direction). Here Willard's *Divine Conspiracy* also instructs me. In it, he described what I've found to be true time and again:

> As I listen, [people] do not have to protect themselves from me, and they begin to open up. I may quickly begin to appear to them as a possible ally and resource. Now they [may] begin to sense their problem to be the situation they have created, or possibly themselves. Because I am no longer trying to drive them, genuine communication, real sharing of hearts, becomes an attractive possibility.[21]

Karen and Patty will never change their lifestyles because I've developed some brilliant argument against homosexuality or for conventional marriage. They certainly won't be motivated to analyze or alter their choices because I turn every conversation into another opportunity to explain "the truth" about their situation (or worse, haphazardly foist a Bible verse on them).

But as I allow them to express and explore what they think, feel, and experience, Karen and Patty may be able to see their decisions for what they are—broken means of grabbing hold of life. If I can be a friend and a resource, a Christ-filled presence in their daily lives, perhaps I can be of some use to the Spirit who wants to woo and win their hearts.

Our society is far beyond the point where mere talk (including the biblical-sounding phrase "hate the sin; love the sinner") can make a lasting difference. We must *choose to live* in such a way that Christ's love through us becomes attractive, magnetic, and desirable.

I once heard author and speaker John Eldredge ask an audience what the problem was with these words from 1 Peter 3:15: "Quietly trust yourself to Christ your Lord, and if anybody asks why you believe as you do, be ready to tell him, and do it in a gentle and respectful way" (TLB). "It's the Bible," I silently argued with him. "There's no problem with it!" But then he floored me with the declaration, "The problem is that *nobody asks*."

I want Patty and Karen to ask why I believe what I do. I plan to be ready to tell them in a gentle and respectful way. I yearn to quietly trust myself to Christ my Lord, living such a life of magnetic love that not only Patty and Karen but everyone who believes and lives differently than I do would be irresistibly drawn to Jesus. Not to my church or to my kind of life, but to Jesus.

While describing my complicated friendship with Patty to my godly mentor, she reminded me that my goal can never be to convert Patty—or anyone else for that matter—to my *lifestyle*. My aim and Christ's command is to direct them to my *Lord*. We're not out to make more disciples of Christianity, but rather lovers of Christ.

Sometimes, however, we get so caught up in trying to perfectly answer the questions that arise because of difficult relationships that we forget we are dealing with *people*, not problems. These questions encompass many situations: "But what about my gay cousin and his partner? Do I invite them to our home for Christmas?" "Is it right to attend the wedding/commitment ceremony of two people you know are living apart from the moral law of God?" "How will I know when to act, to speak, to listen, or to withdraw?" It is important to keep in mind that every situation requires specific guidance, individual discernment. Remember the words of 1 Corinthians 2:14? "Spirit can be known only by spirit—God's Spirit and our spirits in open communion." He alone can direct us through the complexities of each relationship.

Allow me to emphasize, however, that this unique and individual reality of discernment is not a burden but a *freedom*. The fact that there's no formula, no set way, to love people who make choices different from our own is actually a great blessing because we can daily walk with God in creative, life-giving grace that surprises in its cunning and disarms in its manipulation-free innocence.

Of course, the blessing brings with it responsibility (as most blessings do). But I genuinely believe that you'll see, as I have, that exercising discernment in challenging relationships allows us to incarnate—tenderly and powerfully—the God we long to reveal.

The life we crave and the relationships we crave are inextricably bound together. I'm willing to strive with the Spirit's help toward a life of forgiveness, honest evaluation, and noncontriving love. Join me, and let's see our relationships transformed into all that God designed them to be.

Questions for Discussion

1. A husband and wife approached Dr. Emerson Eggerichs for some marital counseling. Eggerichs reported that the "man told me that every time he and his wife got into a fight, she would get 'historical.' To be sure I understood, I asked him if he actually meant 'hysterical.' He said, 'No, historical. She keeps dredging everything up from the past.'"[22] Whether we're single or married, many of us are experts at getting historical. How can forgiveness help us to resist dredging up the past, not only in our conversations, but in the unverbalized thoughts of our minds and feelings of our hearts?

2. Think about a difficult relationship in your life. Without sharing details that would compromise the other person's identity, process with the group (or in a journal entry if you're on your own) how

honestly evaluating this person can help you tenderly and truthfully incarnate Christ to him or her.

3. Take some time to peruse the book of Hosea. In this prophetic
    work, God compares the fidelity Hosea showed to his adulterous
    wife, Gomer, to His own faithful love for Israel. Hosea chapter 2
    clearly reveals that faithfulness includes a forceful refusal to let sin
    continue and a genuine tenderness and mercy that woos unfaithful
    ones to the love they actually crave. How does God's example chal-
    lenge us to act in relationships with people who make poor (if not
    downright sinful) choices? What are some specific ways you can
    love tenderly while refusing to condone sin?

Thoughts for Personal Meditation

Jesus once exposed the hypocrisy of religious men who wouldn't be
caught dead befriending "sinners." Christ lamented, "I, the Messiah,
feast and drink, and you complain that I am 'a glutton and a drinking
man, and hang around with the worst sort of sinners!' But brilliant men
like you can justify your every inconsistency!" (Matthew 11:19, TLB).
Think of a time when you've justified, or have been tempted to justify,
a judgmental or condemnatory attitude toward someone whose lifestyle
differs from your own. Can the truths we explored in this chapter give
you a vision for how the situation might have gone differently had you
shown Christ's incarnating love?

A Prayer to Spark Your Conversation with God

*Father, You use my heart and hands to embrace the world. Thank
You, Lord, for sending me out to touch the world with Your love. In*

the process, I'm reminded that Your love is always there for me, filling me up when I feel empty, healing me when I feel broken, giving my life value and meaning. Help me remember that the love You pour out on my life can be shared, even with people who are very different from me. I confess that I haven't been perfectly faithful to You or to the people You've placed in my life. I've been disrespectful and unforgiving and have judged harshly when grace was needed. Forgive me, Lord, and create a clean heart within me. Search me and reveal any patterns of lovelessness in my relationships. Today I commit myself to love as You have loved. When I share with the hurting and sinful, may Your grace be gloriously revealed. In the holy and powerful name of Jesus, my beloved Savior, amen.[23]

EIGHT

The Church

DISCERNING YOUR ROLE IN THE BODY OF CHRIST

AMBER AND I MET in fourth grade Sunday school. Bright, fun, and the only girl besides me who liked to play with school supplies more than Barbies (perhaps you underestimate how much joy a stapler can give certain nine-year-olds), Amber quickly became a favorite friend. As we grew older, our hearts consistently stirred at the same things, most especially deep conversations about faith and mystery.

Over the two decades I've known Amber, I've continually observed how the Holy Spirit not only helps her think intently and profoundly about her own faith and how it manifests itself in the day-to-day world but also uses her to push others in the same direction.

I hope as Amber shares some of her journey, particularly decisions about her role in the body of Christ, you'll feel encouraged and challenged.

Cultural, Historical, Personal, or Biblical?

While I was growing up, my parents were (and still are) stateside missionaries. I know most people think of missionaries in remote jungles or destitute orphanages, but my life as a missionary kid was pretty normal by American standards, and my first experiences with church were a lot like those of other "raised in Christian homes" girls.

My family attended a large nondenominational church and, as a child, I learned my Bible verses, got the stickers, and sat through scads of flannelgraph story times. As I grew older, I became part of the youth-group leadership team and went on short-term mission trips to Mexico. But during high school, I also started to feel disillusioned by certain church dynamics.

Around the same time, and with the excited sanction of our church staff, my parents launched a house church. Their primary intention was to draw in people who may never have entered the door of a church building. I was eager both to jump into this adventure and to get away from the frustrations of church politics, so toward the end of my senior year I made a deal with my parents: I would attend traditional church twice a month and the other two Sundays I'd worship with them at home.

Our house church included another family and often a few friends or visitors, some of whom knew little, if anything, about Jesus and Christianity. It was kind of refreshing to be around people who didn't have the perfectly packaged Sunday-school answers.

I, on the other hand, had been molded by the language and mores of a very distinct culture. Just as a native Indonesian is powerfully influenced by the traditions of those islands, I'd been profoundly shaped by the late-twentieth-century Christian culture of evangelicalism. At eighteen, I stepped outside that microcosm for the first time.

And as I moved further away from its customs and my learned way of "doing church," I realized just how dissatisfied I'd become with parts of the Christian subculture — the holy-huddle mentality, the Christianese that defined so much of the speech, and the way Bible stories were turned into propositions with three points and an application.

Please understand me: Within the church I grew up attending, there were and still are many passionate followers of Jesus, people who want to incarnate His gospel in the real world. I in no way mean to attack my particular church or the other churches I've visited that share some of the same tendencies.

I simply found myself yearning for more than what the mainline Christian culture seemed to offer. I now recognize that part of the longing sprang from my artist's and writer's heart, which was eager to find my place in the greater story of faith that extends all the way from Abraham to me.

The living, breathing, sinning, doubting, and forgiven characters of Scripture had become two-dimensional abstractions to me rather than fathers of my personal faith. The Christian books I read always seemed to end with a neatly tied up "faith realization" (not to mention a fairy-tale, "she gets the guy" spin). These things just didn't ring true with the world I started to experience as a young adult — a world of pain and mystery and hard questions.

I actually started to envy my friends who left the Christian culture, even those who did so to party it up in college. I'm so grateful God saved me from throwing myself into something other than Him during that time. He graciously placed me in a small-group Bible study with a group of people who hadn't grown up in the evangelical subculture.

These wise new friends urged me not to abandon tradition simply because of its flaws. Within that community of mostly "non-native"

Christians, I saw that cultural mores aren't inherently bad. Only when they become sacred—or, even more insidiously, when they replace the Sacred—does danger arise.

The experiences with my parents' house church and this Bible study gave me both a deeper ownership of my faith and a commitment to wrestle with, rather than simply criticize and discard, the aspects of church life that I started to see were cultural, historical, and traditional, but possibly not biblical.

The idea that Jesus taught about the kingdom of God (a concept I could barely define at the time) but not about a particular way of "doing church" also challenged me profoundly. More and more, I wanted to be an apprentice to Jesus in the larger culture. I began looking for ways to intentionally incarnate Him in the everyday world, not merely in my Christian bubble.

For me, that meant really searching out what the ekklesia—the "called-out ones"—are to do. Ekklesia is the biblical word we've translated into "church," but it originally had less to do with services and methods of worship than it did being set apart and obviously different from the world. From my understanding, it means learning to articulate and live out what the kingdom of God actually is.

It also means purposefully developing relationships with people who don't know Jesus, while at the same time remaining part of a community with whom I can journey deep into the heart of God and into my own depravity, a community in which God can expose the strategies I've concocted for living apart from Him.

Basically, as I've grown and changed, I've seen that my place within the local church and the global church (the body of Christ spread abroad in the world) extends far beyond attending Sunday services at a particular building.

But the road has been, in some respects, a difficult one. Making choices to "do church" in what many view as nontraditional ways has brought a good deal of heartache with it. People's reactions, misunderstanding, and judgment have wounded me, sometimes deeply.

When I was growing up, not "going to church" equaled walking away from God. If you missed three Sundays in a row, people thought you were really backsliding. And according to these same people, spending intentional yet nonspiritually focused time with unbelievers would corrupt you.

But this attitude leaves little, if any, room for taking part in a church community beyond the four walls of a particular building, a community in which being simultaneously called out and a light on the hill is taken seriously. This attitude leaves little room for people like me.

I've wrestled over and over with these questions: What percentage of my faith and my experience with church is cultural? How much is historical and traditional? And how much is genuinely biblical?

More than anything, I want to grow in discipleship with Christ. I want to be part of His ekklesia in the real world. This makes fellowshipping with other believers—the deep life-sharing fellowship the Bible describes—and incarnating Jesus to the hurting world the primary values that drive my choices about church.

What convictions guide your decisions about church?

An Adventure Different from My Own

In many ways, Amber and I are like two peas in a pod. But our journeys with and in the church have diverged radically. As a pastor's wife and youth-group leader, my life is firmly grounded in the traditional church. Still, Amber and I share a deep desire to make wise and thoughtful decisions about our role in church, the Christian culture, and ultimately the entire world.

Both of us recognize the absolute biblical imperative that states, "You should not stay away from the church meetings, as some are doing, but you should meet together and encourage each other. Do this even more as you see the day coming" (Hebrews 10:25, NCV). But what "church meetings" look like for Amber and me differs.

I share Amber's story with you for a couple of reasons. First, I want to debunk the myth that there's one right way to do church. Second, by contrasting her journey with my own, I hope to show that making thoughtful decisions about church means neither that you must ditch the Christian culture because of its flaws nor that you must stick with tradition until death.

In each person's journey of discernment, it's absolutely imperative that he or she explore thoughts and questions about the church. Today, so many people are making decisions about fellowship and worship without really thinking about them. For instance, it currently seems incredibly (and sadly) popular to criticize the church. Some of the most recent Christian best sellers have been about what's wrong with the church and why. The self-corrective potential of evangelicalism can be a beautiful thing, but when it's done indiscriminately, critiquing the church can lead people to treat Christianity more like a product to be consumed or rejected than a personal journey with God. We need discernment to separate unhealthy criticism from authentic challenge.

One blessing of the ongoing evaluation and analysis of Christian culture is that more people (like Amber) are finding their place within the global body of Christ and in communities of genuine Christian faith. But here's the challenge: When people differ in their approach to church, tensions can mount.

I believe that God's Spirit sometimes directs people toward new ways (or ancient ways infused with new life) of "doing church." I grieve when others react to the winds of change with knee-jerk fear. We need discernment to determine when, why, and how to reform church dynamics appropriately.

In 1914, English scholar Evelyn Underhill wrote words about the church that echo into this century. She observed,

Those who cling to tradition and fear all novelty in God's relation with His world deny the creative activity of the Holy Spirit, and forget that what is now tradition was once innovation: that the real Christian is always a revolutionary. . . . In the Church too this process of renovation from within, this fresh invasion of Reality, must constantly be repeated if she is to escape the ever-present danger of stagnation. . . . Thus loyalty to the supernatural calling will mean flexibility to its pressures and demands, and also a constant adjustment to that changing world to which she brings the unchanging gifts. But only insofar as her life is based on prayer and self-offering will she distinguish rightly between these implicits of her vocation and the suggestions of impatience or self-will.[1]

Christian researchers have predicted or pointed out that a genuine revolution is taking place in the church. And, as this quote so beautifully illustrates, we need not fear the creative activity of the Holy Spirit. Without His redeeming work, the church would die (likely from self-inflicted wounds).

As Underhill pointed out, flexibility and constant adjustment do not mean that what the church offers to our world changes but merely that as the world changes (which it inevitably does), God's unchanging grace takes new forms.

But here we find the key: Only in prayer and in presenting herself as an offering can the church separate rightly what is inherently her role and what is the selfish impulse of fleshly desire. Only with discernment can the church change well, determining God's will for today and tomorrow. Only with discernment can we discover our individual roles in the eternal and "ever-transforming to become like Him" body of Christ.

In identifying what God's unchanging purposes for the church are and then candidly exposing some of the ways self-will threatens the body of Christ, I believe we can make decisions about how to "do church" in a way that is both revolutionary and timeless.

In this chapter I want us to exercise discernment by thinking about the decisions we've already made in regard to our local church and the global church. I want to prepare us to discern well in the future. And I pray that conversing about and challenging some of the current trends in the Christian culture will lead us closer to the life we crave.

Set Apart to Display His Goodness

An important decision God asks us to make about church involves determining what the church really is. In his book *Body Life: The Church Comes Alive*, Ray Stedman rightly noted, "God's first concern is not what the church does, it is what the church is. Being must always precede doing, for what we do will be according to what we are."[2] Likewise, we will act within the church according to what we believe it is.

As Amber mentioned, the Greek word we translate "church" is *ekklesia*, a derivative of the particle *ek*, meaning "out," and the verb *kalein*, "to call." Literally rendered, the noun form *ekklesia* is "the called-out ones."

The fundamental meaning of church in the New Testament is a group of people summoned out of something and into something else. But the Bible doesn't stop there; it also reveals out of and to what the church is called. According to 1 Peter 2:9, the church is "a kingdom of priests, God's holy nation, his very own possession. This is so you [the *ekklesia*] can show others the goodness of God, for he called you out of the darkness into his wonderful light" (NLT). Peter taught us here that God calls people *out of* darkness and *into* His wonderful light. Also, we learn that God established the church, the called-out ones, for two reasons: first, so they can be His "very own possession" and second, so they can "show others the goodness of God."

I find N. T. Wright's words on this subject particularly enlightening. In *Simply Christian*, he explained what the Bible clearly communicates:

> [The church] doesn't exist in order to provide a place where people can . . . develop their own spiritual potential. Nor does it exist in order to provide a safe haven in which people can hide from the wicked world and ensure that they themselves arrive safely at an otherworldly destination. Private spiritual growth and ultimate salvation come rather as the byproducts of the . . . overarching purpose for which God has called and is calling us. . . . Through the church God will announce to the wider world that he is indeed its wise, loving, and just creator; that through Jesus he has defeated the powers that corrupt and enslave it; and that by his Spirit he is at work to heal and renew it. . . . From the very beginning, in Jesus's own teaching, it has been clear that people who are called to be agents of God's healing love, putting the world to rights, are called also to be people whose own lives are put to rights by the same healing love.[3]

I'll be the first to confess that I've often thought of the church as a place where people—more specifically *I*—can discover and develop a personal relationship with God ("spiritual potential," as Wright put it). Perhaps less often, but certainly sometimes, I've viewed church as a place where people can be saved from the "wicked world," ensured that they will land on the "right side" at the end of their lives.

What a difference it makes to look at church as an organic reality that announces that God actually is who He claims to be. Church isn't merely a place or a weekly service. God calls individuals out so He can dwell in them, putting them—and through them, the entire world—right with healing love. I can get excited about that vision of church.

And if God truly is calling people out of darkness and into light (which He *is*), if He is genuinely concerned about healing sick individuals with love (which He *is*), a wise description I once read becomes incredibly important: The church is not a museum for saints but a hospital for sinners.[4] In any hospital you'll find people at various stages of sickness, recovery, and healing. Churches should be no different. The old and young, maturing and stagnant, hurting and hopeless should all be able to find their place within the church.

Why is it that many people prefer church to be a comfortable social club instead, a place for others who think and live like them? For some, the thought that people in their church might struggle with homosexuality or drug addiction is a horror. But where are gays and addicts to find God if not in His church?

God didn't create the church to be a holy huddle where Christians safely fellowship with only like-minded people. Through His grace, the church is a fellowship of people who become *family*, a community of faith that joins God in what He wants to do as well as what He's already doing.

When men and women discern what being part of the called-out ones *actually* means, they make the most important decision about church that they can. Sadly, many haven't been informed of the need to make this essential and foundational choice.

But we *must choose*: Will we see the church as an organic body created by God in which we may participate, a body through which God is proclaimed and in which healing love transforms everyday people? Or will we see church as something we do for a few hours on Sunday (and maybe one other night of the week)?

In the book of Acts, we clearly see that the church is *not* just a place to go but an authentically rich and communal life through which Christians can be involved in God's work and others' lives. As Henri Nouwen described it, church then becomes a "community of faith in which there is little to defend but much to share."[5]

Tragically, church more often becomes a place where people feel the need to defend themselves from the attacks of the world or the Enemy, even one another. For many, the term *church* brings such negative images and memories to mind that embracing the biblical concept of church that we've been discussing here seems virtually impossible. For these people, church means a building in which, or a group of people by whom, they've been wounded or rejected. For others, rank hypocrisy and pride poison the word *church*.

I understand these experiences. I've had my share of negative feelings about the church, and much of my ministerial life is about helping people overcome the heinous ways the word *church* has been used and abused.

Some people want to discard the term *church* altogether. But I would rather we *decide* to rethink and reestablish what being the church really means than try to adopt a new descriptive phrase like "the family of God's people" or "those who believe in and follow Jesus." Ditching a term is a Band-Aid solution.[6] Exercising discernment is the better way. Discernment can forge the road between abandoning church altogether and mindlessly following the current of our sometimes exclusive, sometimes hypocritical Christian culture.

As we grab hold of the idea that church actually is something broader and greater and more wonderful than we can possibly imagine—a story in which we can find ourselves as daughters of Eve and children of Abraham, as Esthers who courageously protect their people but still feel fear (see Esther 4:4), as Sarahs tempted to laugh at God's promises but who nonetheless live in faith and do what is right (see 1 Peter 3:6), as *called-out ones* who take seriously their role to incarnate Christ to a world desperate for His healing love—we can start making other decisions about church.

With discernment, we can reestablish a vision for church that, instead of stopping at bitter criticism, goes on to inspire, encourage, and challenge. For instance, we can evaluate not only the consumerism infecting God's church but also how making *wise choices* can positively counteract this trend.

iChurch[7]

In our options-crazy culture, people exalt willpower above all else: Some imagine that they can choose everything, including how church "meets their needs." As a consumer mentality spreads through the church, we find that people want to customize their church experience like they do the playlist on an iPod.

In a penetrating article for *Leadership Journal*, pastor Skye Jethani wrote, "For consumers, fulfillment of desire is the highest good and final arbiter in making decisions—even deciding where [and I would add how] to worship." Jethani described a conversation he had with two former members of his congregation. Apparently these folks told Pastor Jethani they had decided to attend another church. He wrote,

> *During my conversation with Greg and Margaret at Starbucks, I asked how they came to choose Faith Community as their new church. "Did you pray as a family about this decision?" No. "Did you involve your small group or seek the wisdom of an elder in the decision?" No. "Did you investigate the church's doctrine, history, or philosophy of ministry?" No. "Did you base your decision on anything other than what you 'liked'?" No.*

Jethani described Greg and Margaret as an educated, professional couple capable of making intelligent decisions. He also noted, however, that "being fully formed in a consumer worldview, Greg and Margaret intuitively accepted that the personal enrichment and fulfillment of desire is the highest good. As a result, they chose the church that best satisfied their family's preferences. . . . After all, in consumerism a desire is never illegitimate, it is only unmet."[8]

How many people do you know who have chosen a church principally because of felt needs? Maybe because they like the worship better here or because the youth programs over there provide more of what their kids enjoy.

While desire certainly forms part of the decision to participate in a community of faith, when "my/our needs" are the primary or only determinants, church wrongly becomes more about personal fulfillment (remember N. T. Wright's words, "a place where people can . . . develop their own spiritual potential") than God's purposes.

And though what authors Roger Finke and Rodney Stark pointed out in *The Churching of America, 1776–1990* is true, their observations are also a bit frightening. Finke and Stark argued that ministry in the U.S. follows a primarily capitalist model, with pastors functioning as a church's sales force and evangelism as its marketing strategy. From Finke and Stark's research, it's clear that the American church first began to adopt this consumer-driven model after the First Amendment separated church and state.[9] Like the purchasing of (or the decision not to purchase) material goods, faith became largely a matter of personal choice. Churches naturally started vying for members, implementing promotional stratagems, and developing secular business values.

Skye Jethani noted with evident sadness that churches today are

> in competition with other providers of identity and meaning for survival. We [pastors of particular congregations] must convince a sustainable segment of the religious marketplace that our church is 'relevant,' 'comfortable,' or 'exciting.' (One billboard in my area proclaims, 'Kids love our church. It's FUN!') . . . We must differentiate our church by providing more of the elements people want. After all, in a consumer culture, the customer is king.[10]

It's absolutely true: In the marketplace, consumers demand options. People see choice as their right. At fast-food joints you can always "have it your way." And at Starbucks, you can select a beverage from over twenty thousand permutations. To think, I viewed their menu as a pretty simple one.

But for the church, the "customer is king/I want it my way" mentality poses *major problems*. The primary functions of the church that we saw in 1 Peter 2:9 just don't fit with the "I've got a right to . . ." attitude of consumerist churchgoing. Spiritual formation, for instance, cannot be accomplished strictly by getting what we want.

Scott McKinney, a good friend and great pastor on the frontlines in Central Utah, recently told me, "There are churches where you can literally choose between island rhythms, country, or rock-and-roll worship. But that's not going to be us. It's okay for our young people to struggle through a hymn now and then. It's all right for our older folks to wrestle with a new style. People constantly underestimate what happens when they engage with what makes them uncomfortable rather than simply avoid it."

In a choice-crazed society, where we imagine the only worth something (even someone) has is the value we assign it, participating in the church becomes a "What can it do for me?" pursuit. Christianity can be demoted from a life to a label. And if church "isn't doing anything for me," I'll allocate it little time, energy, or passion.

In 2005, University of North Carolina sociologist Christian Smith published the results of his five-year study on the spiritual lives of American teenagers. Smith concluded that even among those who attend evangelical churches, the faith of young people in the United States is MTD: Moralistic Therapeutic Deism. Smith wrote,

Moralistic Therapeutic Deism is about belief in a particular kind of God: one who exists, created the world, and defines our general

moral order, but not one who is particularly personally involved in [our] affairs — especially affairs in which one would prefer not to have God involved. Most of the time, the God of this faith keeps a safe distance. . . . God sometimes does get involved in people's lives, but usually only when they call on him, mostly when they have some trouble or problem or bad feeling that they want resolved. In this sense, the Deism here is revised from the classical eighteenth-century version by the therapeutic qualifier, making the distant God selectively available for taking care of needs. This God is not demanding. He actually can't be, because his job is to solve our problems and make people feel good. In short, God is something like a combination Divine Butler and Cosmic Therapist.[11]

If you've taken time to observe the faith that adult members of your local church exhibit, you may likely agree with me: This trend among teens extends far beyond adolescence.

Among the tragic results of Moralistic Therapeutic Deism, church becomes merely an adjunct to daily life: What matters most is what the congregation provides for me (or my kids or my elderly parents or so on).

And if, as it seems, our contemporary Christian culture is quickly spiraling toward the logical conclusion of consumer faith — iChurch — we must first stem this tide in our own minds and lives, exercising our God-given discernment to do so. Instead of asking, "What is this church doing for me?" perhaps we can consider questions such as, "Is there a church — whether a conventional congregation or a home church community like the kind Amber takes part in — that I can join my life with? Is there a body of believers with whom I can grow into my role as part of God's set-apart people and show others the goodness of God (see 1 Peter 2:9)? If so, will I then commit to refraining from any murmuring against the church of God?"

As I mentioned before, criticizing the church is quite popular these days. Some undiscerning readers take best-selling books that analyze Christian culture to mean that the local church is broken beyond repair. Others begin to murmur. Dr. Joseph Stowell discussed murmuring in his book *The Weight of Your Words*. He wrote, "Murmuring is a form of complaining that harbors a negative attitude toward a situation or the people involved."[12] Stowell also showed how murmuring distorts good judgment by focusing on the self (for example, how I've been mistreated, misunderstood, or let down).

There is no doubt: Many, if not most people, have experienced deep wounds at the hands of churchgoing folk. There are some churches who, for lack of a better phrase, "shoot their own." The mistakes made by churches across the world and across the centuries echo painfully in the memories of many men and women. But as the apostle James might well have said to us today, "My friends, *this can't go on*" (James 3:10, emphasis added).

If we decide to live out what God teaches us about being set apart and living as set-apart ones (in but not of the world), we *will* find that unselfishly participating in the church becomes a natural and joyful outgrowth of our growing fellowship with Jesus.

Those focused on God's glory, not strictly their own pleasure, can view the problems in a church with discernment. They can choose not to grumble or murmur, even if they determine that God is calling them to join another body of believers. If they desire to make a change, they ask the Spirit to reveal their motives. In other words, they are in continual personal conversation with God about their role in and outside of their specific church, as well as the global church.

They see church, as Brennan Manning's book *The Ragamuffin Gospel* describes, as "a place of promise and possibility, of adventure and discovery, a community of compassion on the move. . . . In their community worship, they reject the insidious inclination to play it safe.

[Instead], the inveterate tendency to entrenchment, which betrays itself in clinging to the tried and true, is accurately discerned as a sign of distrust in the Holy Spirit."[13]

Discernment helps us navigate between robotically "clinging to the tried and true" (aka distrusting the Holy Spirit) and making church about our needs. Discernment simultaneously enables us to avoid entrenchment and consumerism. And it does so by engaging us—Spirit to spirit—in open, continual, and personal communion with God.

The Role of "How I Feel"

In light of all we've discussed, it's important that we now explore the role emotions, desire, and experience play in making decisions about church. After reading the previous section, some readers may mistakenly believe that to avoid consumerism, I'd advocate sticking with a church no matter what its problems, how a person feels about what goes on in the congregation, or what someone desires in his or her fellowship with other believers. This certainly is *not* my intention.

Because of the amazingly unique way God fashions each of us, I believe He also offers us many ways to worship Him within a community of faith. And part of the way we determine which body of believers to join our lives with is by discerning what our emotions, longings, and experiences reveal about who God made us to be.

My parents are good examples of this. Like Amber, I grew up in a large nondenominational church. For over fifteen years, my parents attended worship services there that were filled with great music and outstanding teaching. They also grew intimate with a small-group fellowship called Joint Heirs. My folks truly blended their lives with other members of the congregation and, though I'm perhaps a bit biased by love, I believe my mom and dad genuinely sought to live out the purposes of the church—to be set apart and to reveal goodness to the world.

Some time after I left home, my parents felt drawn to worship in new ways. For instance, they earnestly desired to take communion more frequently. They'd also learned some liturgical prayers and felt excited by the connection with tradition and communion with the saints of old that liturgy offered. After visiting Blessed Sacrament, a small Episcopal parish close to their home, my parents found that their spirits resonated deeply with the traditions there. Over a period of a year and some months, my mom and dad wrestled with whether they should stay at the church where they'd put down so many roots or move on. They knew the risks: Others (especially those who view Episcopalians as heathens) might misunderstand their longing to worship in a different way, friendships would change, and they might not be doing the "right" thing.

But through a great deal of prayer and asking for guidance, my parents decided to join their lives with the body of believers at Blessed Sacrament. A much smaller community of faith than the one they previously participated in, the parish in which they now serve and live out their faith offers some of the things that nourish my parents most at this stage of their lives. And both of them can serve, my dad in the music department, my mom with her gifts of hospitality, and together as mentors for a small group of young married couples.

Discernment makes all the difference when determining how God calls each individual to worship and serve Him within a church. An undiscerning decision to go where our needs are met is different from genuinely asking God to guide us. He wants us to be where we can most fully experience Him and participate in His church, but because that may be different from what we imagine (or believe we need), discernment is imperative.

I believe that if the Holy Spirit had so directed them, my parents would have stayed at the larger evangelical church they attended for so many years. But after thoughtfully and prayerfully examining their desires, their emotions, and their experiences, my parents genuinely believed that God was leading them in a new adventure within the church.

It does no good to steadfastly remain in a congregation while progressively experiencing less of God. When anything, including a particular way of "doing church," comes between "the primary experience of Jesus as the Christ, we become unconvicted and unpersuasive travel agents handing out brochures to places we have never visited."[14]

Only experiencing personal communion with God will enable us to fulfill the purposes for which we are called out. As philosopher Jacques Maritain once described, for the Christian, "the culmination of knowledge is not conceptual but experiential: I feel God. Such is the promise of the Scriptures: Be still and know (experience) that I am God."[15] If we are to genuinely reveal the goodness of God to the world, we must feel what we know about God. If a church fails to promote the foundational goals of the called-out ones, people will feel themselves withering instead of thriving. How we feel about church and God matters a lot.

At the same time, we cannot view our experience of God as an emotional encounter of only *one kind*. As author Gordon T. Smith observed, if music is used to manipulate the emotions and if the liturgy no longer becomes focused on giving life but rather on escaping from it, what churchgoers have is not worship but the "experience of a feeling." An "emotional package" begins to replace the living presence of God.[16]

Discernment helps us recognize when we've substituted an emotional experience with church for authentic communion with God. And though genuinely entering the presence of God within a fellowship of believers *will* be accompanied by emotion, we may need to be trained to recognize the reverent awe, humble gratitude, overwhelming love, or quiet, almost unperceivable feeling that stillness before Him often produces.

The tension we find is that God neither intends for us to rely completely on our desires or emotions about church (whether we experience Him in a particular way or during a specific service) nor commands us to abandon these concerns altogether. As with many things, He invites us to exercise discernment in distinguishing what is of Him, what stems from our broken will, and what comes from the Enemy of our souls.

I like what Dr. John Coe, director of Talbot Theological Seminary's school of spiritual formation, teaches: Discernment helps us determine what our feelings reveal about the state of our hearts. When people endure a Sunday service without the slightest desire to worship, when they try to practice corporate spiritual disciplines (study, prayer, or silence) and sense themselves agitated and confused, Coe encourages them to stop berating themselves for not feeling the "right way" and instead to ask God what their souls are communicating.

It requires great discernment to navigate the tension between our alternating desires about church. As we discussed at length in chapter 2, we can neither follow our hearts indiscriminately nor ignore our feelings—even the messiest of them—altogether. The longings and emotions in our hearts about the global church or a specific church may reveal that we've been wounded and can choose to forgive, that we've been selfish and can repent, or that we've traded intimacy with Jesus for unswerving devotion to a certain religious experience, congregation, or building. God's Spirit may communicate something entirely different through your emotions about church. *He* will guide you on the journey of discernment. *He* will reveal what your experience is expressing and how much you should listen to the feelings and desires of your heart.

Ask God to reveal specifically what the desires, emotions, and experiences you have at church or when thinking about church mean. Often, though we genuinely want to know God's will, we fail to very directly and explicitly ask Him. Sometimes a simple first step like this can be lost in the enormity of our open-ended questioning: *What do*

You want me to do, Lord? Plainly asking God, *What does this desire to fellowship in a different church mean?*, *What is it about this service that irritates me?*, or other specific questions like these will help you discern not only what to do but also what thoughts come from you, God, and/or the Enemy.

I hope that as we close this chapter, you've begun to think through some of the ways people's understanding of church can be traditional but not biblical, how consumerism has infected nearly everyone's attitudes toward "doing church," and the role desire, emotion, and experience play in decisions about church.

Perhaps the ideas we've discussed have given rise to some questions or longings you didn't even know you had. I pray you'll take anything that sparked your interest (or anything you feel I left out, since this chapter is certainly not a comprehensive discussion of God's church) and journey further and deeper with the Holy Spirit. And may God bless you as you do so.

Questions for Discussion

1. Why do you think it's difficult for churches, especially the people who make up church congregations, to change? Why do you think some people prefer churches that bear a greater resemblance to museums for saints than hospitals for sinners? What thoughts and emotions does this idea bring up: Your church is just the right place for addicts, homosexuals, and others in need of transforming love?

2. Do you agree with my assertion that "if, as it seems, our contemporary Christian culture is quickly spiraling toward the logical conclusion of consumer faith—iChurch—we must first stem this tide in our own minds and lives, exercising our God-given discernment

to do so"? What two practical ways of working this out can you commit to? What about your group as a whole?

3. Modern Christians seem especially hungry for a transcendent experience at church. I have often wondered if this is because fewer and fewer people are taking the time and investing the energy to be still and know God on their own. What do you think of this idea? Are you ever tempted to trade religious experience for knowing God? What about to ignore or discount your desires and emotions altogether? Why? What do you think of the suggestion to ask God specific questions regarding what your longings and feelings reveal about your heart? Do you think this will help you make better decisions about church? Why or why not?

Thoughts for Personal Meditation

In *The Weight of Your Words*, Dr. Joseph Stowell related the story of a Christian doctor and his family. When Stowell learned that all of this man's children were grown, committed to Christ, and fellowshipping in a community of faith, Stowell, a father of three, wanted to know the secret to his success in raising kids. The doctor credited God's grace and added that he and his wife made a decision very early on that their children would never hear them complain about or criticize their church, church leaders, or another brother or sister in Christ. Stowell appropriately observed that we don't often acknowledge how our murmuring against the church influences others.[17] Can you think of a time when you've criticized the church or another Christian in front of someone else? If so, ask God to take you back to that instance and reveal what was going on in your heart and mind at the time. How might your comment have affected the way that person understands church? Is God asking you to make any commitment about murmuring in the future?

A Prayer to Spark Your Conversation with God

Gracious Father, I pray for the global church and for my particular church. "Fill it with all truth, in all truth with all peace. Where it is corrupt, purify it; where it is in error, direct it; where in any thing it is amiss, reform it. Where it is right, strengthen it; where it is in want, provide for it; where it is divided, reunite it; for the sake of Jesus Christ thy Son our Savior. Amen."[18]

NINE

Discerning Faith

A LIFE TO BE ENJOYED

DURING CHILDHOOD, I WAS what you might call a spiritual sponge. I soaked up pretty much whatever people told me about God, myself, and faith. I was also deeply committed to our church, part of a religious tradition that extended five generations back on both sides of my family.

When my parents told me they no longer believed the leaders of this church were prophets, I knew I had some very important and difficult choices to make. But I was only eight years old, and answers did not come as readily as questions: Should I abandon faith altogether? Could I ever fully embrace another set of teachings that claimed to be the only truth? What should I do with the Bible — can I trust it? And who is God really?

By the time I turned twelve, I had read through many of the teachings of my extended family's church, as well as the entire Bible. At that age, I didn't understand everything completely. But I distinctly recall deciding for myself—though I now know this never could have happened without the Holy Spirit's initiative—that I wanted to follow Jesus. For me, that meant rejecting the religious traditions of my ancestors.

I'm so grateful that while my parents studied the Bible and lived out their faith in Jesus, they taught me about discerning faith. As my mom trained younger children at our new church to discern between Truth and lies using God's Word as a plumb line (see Amos 7:7-8), I listened intently. And both my parents emphasized the importance of determining what God's truth, goodness, and beauty look like in the real world.

Still, my first experiences with religion continued to affect me deeply. For instance, the church I previously attended taught that the Holy Spirit would leave if I was bad, an idea that terrified me and definitely contributed to my lifelong struggle with perfectionism. Because I had fervently believed this and other distortions of the truth about God or myself, some of the choices I made during and after my adolescent conversion, decisions about whom and what I could trust, are still unfolding to this day.

Perhaps more than some, I've been forced to exercise discernment in matters of faith. I've had to consciously determine, again and again, what to believe or reject about myself, God, and what authentically walking with Him looks like. But I am genuinely glad about and deeply grateful for the experiences of my life. Though I certainly don't wish on anyone the division my parents' (and to some extent my own) conversion caused in our extended family or the profound pain that came with it, I do pray that every person would be brought to a place like I was—a place where he or she could learn to discern in matters of faith.

Beginning a Vigorous Search

Whether you grew up in a Christian home or converted from another religion like I did, each of us has made decisions about faith that have changed the very fabric of our lives. And at one time or another many of us have chosen—whether we were deceived or acting out of rebellion—to believe lies that have poisoned our understanding about the life of authentic faith. Discernment helps us identify these lies and replace them with truth. In this chapter I'd like to explore how discernment can help us sort through the ideas that constantly bombard us about ourselves, God, and what walking with Him looks like.

I earnestly desire to see people make wise decisions about their faith. And the most fundamental area we can learn to practice discernment is in our view of God. If we don't make choices to believe or reject certain things about God, the rest of our "faith" will have little impact on our lives. So let's explore for a moment this question: Who does God reveal Himself to be?

An Infinitely Joyous Love

In his work *The Knowledge of the Holy*, A. W. Tozer wrote,

> *That our idea of God corresponds as nearly as possible to the true being of God is of immense importance to us. . . . Our real idea of God may lie buried under the rubbish of conventional religious notions and may require an intelligent and vigorous search before it is finally unearthed and exposed for what it is. Only after an ordeal of painful self-probing are we likely to discover what we actually believe about God.*[1]

I'll be frank with you. When I first read this quote, "an ordeal of painful self-probing" sounded overwhelming. But as God invited me deep into the corners of my mind, as He helped me probe the recesses of my thoughts about Him—the ones that had been buried under not only the rubbish of traditions and religious notions but also the doubts and fears of my sometimes insecure heart—I discovered that the pain Tozer described here is a redemptive pain, a pain that heals.

It's as if an immense weight, an immense burden, drops off your shoulders.[2] But as experience has probably taught you, once you've carried a heavy load for any significant length of time, releasing the weight can be as difficult and uncomfortable as continuing to lug it around. Still, it is a suffering worth every moment of distress, a grief that leads to greater hope and joy than one could imagine or ask for. This is the kind of redemptive pain that leads to freedom enabling us to probe the depths of what we truly believe about God.

The great burdens that many people carry are the ideas that God is distant from us and that He is a harsh taskmaster we can never please or understand. Also, though it looks a bit sacrilegious when written, we struggle with the idea that God—and life in Him—is dull. Christ invites us to release these heavy loads and know Him as He really is.

The Bible readily reveals that, while here on earth, Jesus manifested a dynamic and contagious joie de vivre. The details of Christ's life, as Dallas Willard pointed out, clearly refute the idea that our God is a "morose and miserable monarch, a frustrated and petty parent, or a policeman on the prowl."[3]

In his book *The Divine Conspiracy*, Willard skillfully exposed other false views we lug around about God. Today, for instance, very few people think of Jesus as an interesting person, let alone someone of vital relevance to the actual events of their everyday lives. Rather than being regarded as a *real-life* personality who deals with *real-life* issues, Jesus is generally thought to be concerned only with the heavenly realm, which is not pertinent to the issues we have to deal with—and deal with *now*. Quite frankly, Willard claimed, Jesus is not considered a person of much ability.[4]

But if we don't fully believe that Jesus is the most interesting and the most *brilliant* human who ever lived, how can we worship Him as Lord? How can we trust Him as the Source of knowledge and understanding? Discerning faith sees God as He really is.

I had never thought of it precisely in these terms, but Willard's book helped me acknowledge that if Jesus is all-knowing, He fully comprehends the nuclear physics that scientists have only recently "discovered." Jesus could explain to you not only how but why Plato came to the philosophical conclusions that he did. Jesus was not merely a person of great ability; He was the person of *greatest ability* who ever lived.[5]

What Christ taught while here on earth, and the truths that resonate in His timeless Word, are not just nice (but otherworldly and irrelevant to the pressing needs of today) sayings. Rather, Jesus communicated a cohesive and brilliantly constructed system of thought, belief, and action that reveals a mind more marvelous and intelligent than I can possibly describe.

Furthermore, Jesus led here on earth, and leads with the Father and Holy Spirit in eternity, a very interesting and full life. He lives with the kind of joyful delight that we constantly crave but only experience in fleeting moments. The most awe-inspiring things I've see here on earth—the breathtaking majesty of the Pacific Ocean crashing on the shores of Maui, the terrifying grandeur of Zugspitze, the first smile of my newborn daughters—are the kinds of glory God sees *all the time.*

God continually experiences the waves of delighted joy that I have felt, the ones I wish so much I could hold on to. "It is perhaps strange to say," Willard wrote after reflecting on this truth, "but suddenly I was extremely happy for God and thought I had some sense of what an infinitely joyous consciousness he is and of what it might have meant for him to look at his creation and find it 'very good.'"[6]

Friends, this is our God—the God revealed by the Bible, the God discernable to humans, the God we can choose to know, love, and serve. He is a God of such ability that *no question* is beyond His understanding, no situation beyond His guidance; and He is a God of such infinitely joyous consciousness that the delight we crave is ever before and with Him. On top of all this, He is a God of unconditionally gracious love.

But the world (and, tragically, sometimes the church) turns the gospel of grace into what Brennan Manning described as "religious bondage," which "distort[s] the image of God into an eternal, small-minded bookkeeper. . . . Put bluntly, the American church today accepts grace in theory but denies it in practice."[7]

Instead of trusting that God, who invites us to call Him Abba (Daddy), loves us because we are His children, we live as if He loves us best—in some people's minds, only—if we are "good little boys and girls." We believe this lie despite the Bible's clear refutation of such a notion. In Colossians 1 we discover,

> *At one time you all had your backs turned to God, thinking rebellious thoughts of him, giving him trouble every chance you got. But now, by giving himself completely at the Cross, actually dying for you, Christ brought you over to God's side and put your lives together, whole and holy in his presence. (verses 21-22)*

When Christ lovingly died to save us, we were the furthest thing from "good little boys and girls." As Romans 5:8 proclaims, "God put his love on the line for us . . . while we were of no use whatever to him." I was of no use whatever to Him; I was giving Him trouble every chance I got; I was thinking rebellious thoughts and carrying out wicked deeds; and at that very moment Christ died for me . . . for you . . . for all of us.

Christ suffered for *love* of us. And He did so not despite our sinfulness but in the very midst of it. He died to save us from eternal ruin and, above all, to win our love. God doesn't want merely our good behavior. He wants the passionate adoration of our hearts.

We'll never appreciate the extraordinary depth of who God is and the kind of love He offers us until we recognize that grace means that God isn't disappointed when we can't get our act together, nor is He waiting to whip us into shape when we get out of line (again). He isn't an eternal scorekeeper who will reveal our point total on judgment day. The full extent of God's grace was poured out for us when we were God's enemies. If He loved us completely and unreservedly when we had our backs turned to Him, what does that say about His love for us?

Though many of us have heard this before, we haven't always chosen to live out of the Truth. Some of us subconsciously reject the thought that God *never* conditions His love on our behavior because that idea just seems too simple. What motivates me or anyone else to be good if God loves us the same at our worst as He does at our best? While this question may profit us some in analyzing why we choose to do good or bad things, it offers little help in facing the darkness in our hearts. If we cannot trust God's love for us implicitly, the ugliness of our sin will simply overpower us.

Instead, God invites us to discern who we really are. His gracious (unmerited, undeserved, but unconditionally given) love for us ensures that we can probe the depths of who we are. And, more important, that we can be healed on that deepest level.

I feel safe with God when I choose to know Him as He really is. Safe enough to venture into the depth of who I am. And this is the next question our journey of discerning faith prompts us to answer: If this is who God is, who are we?

The Disciples Jesus Loves

The simple truth is that the better we know ourselves, the better we'll be able to make wise choices. The more illusions we hold about ourselves, the greater the likelihood that we will not choose well. So coupling discernment and self-evaluation equips us to live well and choose wisely.

In the last section, we explored how God loved us and sent His Son to die for us "while we were still sinners" (Romans 5:8, NCV). If you ask me, the fact that I'm a sinner doesn't sound like particularly good news. Truthfully, it makes me feel pretty worthless. But I love how God, in His infinite goodness, turns this idea on its head. Through His gracious action to save and redeem mankind—over and over again—we see that "even in its ruined condition a human being is regarded by God as something immensely worth saving. *Sin does not make it worthless, but only lost.* And in its lostness it is still capable of great strength, dignity, and heartbreaking beauty and goodness."[8]

What a glorious, freeing truth: Sin does not make me worthless, only lost. Before I knew Christ, I was eternally lost, sinking in the mire of my own woundedness and wickedness. As the great hymn proclaims, "I once was lost, but now am found, was blind but now I see." When I sin now, I momentarily lose my way. I lose track of who I am and where I'm going. But neither before, in my eternally lost condition, nor now, in my temporarily lost one, am I worthless.

Why? Because lostness is not the first nor last word about my identity. The first and most important word about me, and about *you*, is that we are the beloved bearers of God's divine image. As John Eldredge asserted in *Waking the Dead*, we've heard a whole lot about our original sin but not nearly enough about our original glory.[9]

Original glory—I love that phrase.

When "God said, 'Let us make human beings in our image and likeness'" (Genesis 1:26, NCV), He conferred incredible and irrevocable dignity on every person. Beauty and significance, too. And while sin certainly mars the original glory God intended us to reflect, it can *never* destroy or replace it.

Still, most people battle an underlying sense of self-rejection. And as the great contemplative writer Henri Nouwen called it, self-rejection is "the greatest enemy of the spiritual life." Why? "Because it contradicts the sacred voice that calls us the 'Beloved' [and] being the Beloved constitutes the core truth of our existence,"[10] of *your* existence.

A mature, discerning faith certainly encourages us to recognize the depths of our lostness. But it never stops there. Discernment helps us concurrently embrace the truths that we are the objects of God's delight and bearers of original glory.

The apostle John clearly understood this. Did you know that he actually referred to himself as "the disciple Jesus loved"? And that he did so not once, but several times (John 13:23; 20:2; 21:7,20)? While meditating on this chapter of Scripture some time ago, it came to me that John's statement was not born of arrogance or because Jesus showed John some sort of special favoritism (which I sometimes was tempted to think). These ideas simply don't reconcile with the rest of the Bible (see Acts 10:34; Romans 2:11).

Truth hit me like a lightning bolt: John is the disciple Jesus loved, but I am the disciple Jesus loves too. *You* are the disciple Jesus loves as well. John could call himself the disciple Jesus loved because he was absolutely and unashamedly convinced of his belovedness. Oh how I yearn to be that convinced, to trust so deeply in my Savior's love that I might forever and boldly declare myself "the disciple Jesus loves." But let's be honest: It's difficult to grab hold of this truth.

Even G. K. Chesterton, a great man of God, claimed that the hardest thing to believe in the Christian religion is the infinite value it places on the worth of individual persons.[11] I'd have thought that perhaps the doctrine of the Trinity or that of the Resurrection might be more difficult for a keen-minded intellectual like Chesterton to accept.

But no matter what a person's abilities, whether she's at her best writing incisive analyses of theology (as Chesterton seemed to be) or making a mean pot of chicken noodle soup (like some of the women at church who feel they can't do anything for God but actually do amazing things for Him with spices and sauces), the most pressing challenge to our faith often becomes believing in our belovedness.

And by believing, I mean the kind of world-changing, "down to the core of your body and soul" knowledge that transforms every aspect of your life, from the facial expressions that automatically spring onto your features when the checkout clerk at Target frustrates you to the deepest concerns of your heart: "If anyone really knew me, would they love me?"

God answered this question definitively and eternally on a lonely, bloody cross over two thousand years ago. From Calvary, Jesus cried out, "It is finished." Your sin, your shame, the debt of not being good enough was *erased*. What remains is the original glory God is continually repairing in you. What endures is the undeniable beauty and strength and dignity of your belovedness.

But will you embrace this? Will you stretch your arms out and receive? Will you come to Him hungry, *knowing* He will satisfy? Discerning faith separates the truth about who we are from the toxic feelings that threaten us ("I'll never be as godly as *she*," "I'm sure God would love me more if I _____," and on and on and on). Discerning faith lives out the truths that God reveals about Himself and about the irrevocable, infinite worth of *every* individual. A faith that discerns in these matters becomes ready, poised to make wise decisions in other areas as well.

Grace Is the Last Word

To synthesize everything, He is Love and you are loved. If we accept these things, our endless and exhausting attempts to garner His favor, our confused turnings to the broken things of this world that promise us relief from pain, our consuming anxiety about status and position fade into the distance. Strength, disentanglement, and peace become our portion.

I just love Evelyn Underhill's exploration of this idea in her masterful work *Abba*. She wrote,

> *Adoration, a delighted recognition of the life and action of God, . . . is the essential preparation for action. That stops all feverish strain, all rebellion and despondency, all sense of our own importance, all worry about our own success; and so gives dignity, detachment, tranquility to our action and may make it of some use to Him.*[12]

As we've already seen, there are so many things to adore, so many delightful things to recognize about God.

While I was writing this chapter, I discussed with my very good friend Kathy the idea that since God has the full splendor of creation *always* before Him, He must lead an amazingly interesting and joyous life. She brought up this mind-blowing truth to add to the conversation: As much as God enjoys His other creations, just think how much more joy He finds in us, the crown of His creativity. God didn't die to save Mount Everest or the Tahitian sunset, as awesome as they might be. He died for individuals—broken or battered, mean or catty, abused or addicted—who He proclaims are capable of revealing and enjoying greater beauty and goodness than even the most sublime works of nature.

Accepting this reality allows us to discern what walking with God really looks like. It lifts us from the guilt of our past and helps us refute the toxic lie that "God can never forgive me—or even if He can, I can never forgive myself." Living in Truth transforms our present, giving us the serene confidence we desperately long for (and try, in heaven knows how many destructive ways, to secure for ourselves). Genuinely believing the Truth revolutionizes our ability to decide in the future.

Imagine what it would be like for you to make decisions with the *absolute* assurance of God's goodness and love, with the *unqualified* guarantee that you are the beloved. Do you think it might be easier to make certain choices? What if you really believed that the eternal possibility of being forgiven was a more important and foundational truth for decision making than being sure you did the "right thing"? Discerning faith prepares us for action by relieving us of feverish strain and granting us security and hope. It also allows us to risk, to trust that God judges us mercifully, that grace is the last word.

In his book *Emotions: Can You Trust Them?*, Dr. James Dobson made a great analogy to illustrate this point:

> *Suppose I gave my three-year-old son a direct order: "Ryan, please close the door." However, in his childish immaturity he failed to grasp the meaning of my words and opened the door further. He did not obey me. He did the exact opposite of what I commanded. Yet I would be a most unworthy father if I punished him for his failure. He was trying to do what I asked, but his understanding of my request was incomplete. You see, I judge my son more by his intent than by his actual behavior. . . . It is with great comfort that I rest in that same relationship with God. . . . My merciful Father judges me according to the expression of my will.*[13]

Similar scenarios often play out between me and my four-year-old daughter, Jasmine. I ask her to do something, she hears me, and I think, *Great! She's got it.* But then she does something *entirely different* from what I asked. When I correct her, she immediately wants to know, "Are you going to give me a time out? Do you still love me?" The first and most important thing is to assure Jasmine, "Of course I still love you, my Jazzy Jas." But I also need to tell her that I will not discipline her when the motives of her heart were right. And God is infinitely more gracious than I am. If we genuinely desire to honor Him with our decisions, we can trust that He will not capriciously punish us for "getting it wrong."

As Christ renovates us from the inside out, we are *works in progress.* And, as scholar Pierre Wolff pointed out, this

> *unfinished quality of our lives is a blessing. It assures that, if nothing can be perfectly accomplished for and by us here and now, then nothing can be definitively lost or missed, and nothing is totally irreparable. Unfinished means that no death is a dead end. . . . The word unfinished suggests infinite. It is a call to a road never closed and barren, a road wide open to life, to everlasting life.*[14]

Discerning faith recognizes this bottom-line truth: We can always be forgiven. How much we can thank God that our stories are still unfinished! Instead, we sometimes get so caught up in trying to overcome our sin that we lose sight of what really matters. God wants us to look only at Him.

In Luke 7:36-50, during Jesus' dinner at the home of Simon the Pharisee, a sinful woman (many scholars believe Mary Magdalene) washed Jesus' feet with her tears and lavished costly oils on Him. The disciples criticized her for wasting expensive perfume, and the "good religious" folks could not believe Jesus allowed such a woman to touch Him. They scorned her choice and His. Christ, however, affirmed the risky decision of this broken woman. Claude de la Columbiere, a French theologian, observed, "It is certain that of all those present, the one who most honors the Lord is Magdalene, who is so persuaded of the infinite mercy of God that all her sins appear to her as but an atom in the presence of this mercy."[15]

When we truly believe that all our sins are but an atom in His presence, when we choose to risk the opinions of others and even the chance that we might misunderstand God (as my little Jasmine often does me), we become ready to make every decision with greater freedom and confidence.

As we continually live out the *truth* about who God is, who we are, and what His love means for us, our entire life changes. We start experiencing daily what Jesus died to give us—eternal life.

No End and No Limits[16]

Most of us know the words of John 3:16: "God loved the world so much that he gave his one and only Son so that whoever believes in him may not be lost, but have eternal life" (NCV). I don't know how you interpret it, but for a long time, eternal life and heaven were synonymous in my thinking. Eternal, or "everlasting," life (as others have rendered John 3:16's closing words) meant life that went on after death.

But read with me *The Message* translation of John 3:16: "This is how much God loved the world: He gave his Son, his one and only Son. And this is why: so that no one need be destroyed; by believing in him, anyone can have a whole and lasting life."

Isn't that beautiful? Just when we're on the brink of destruction, God offers us "whole and lasting life." That's the kind of life I crave. But honestly, of what use for me *today* is a life—even if it is whole and lasting—that starts after death?

Of course, there probably are many of you who recognize that by equating it with life after death, I completely missed the meaning of "eternal life." Christianity doesn't simply offer people life after they die. The mistaken notion that the point of religion is to wind up in the right place (that is, heaven rather than hell) at the end of the game still holds many people hostage, unable to grab hold of the life they really crave. Discernment helps us experience eternal life *now*, as Christ intended us to.

Eternal life is not merely about duration but also quality—eternal life means life lived to the limit. The real good news is that our eternal life is a life for *now*, not just for later. The gospel is for the living. It's not merely to be accepted today and enjoyed later. It can be entered into presently. Eternal life is a life *now ongoing*.

This means each of us is living—right now—a life that will last forever. And this is the "whole and lasting" life we crave. We long for more than the promise of a "get out of jail free" card, redeemable upon death. We yearn to be part of something greater than ourselves, something beautiful and true and powerful—something *now*.

And we can have this marvelous reality. The moment we enter into relationship with Jesus Christ, a life of joyous and creative participation in God's kingdom—from now through eternity—becomes ours for the taking. Unfortunately, as we do with eternal life, we often misunderstand what God's kingdom is, equating it with an otherworldly realm far from us. Of course God is in the most distant reaches of space (and even beyond space). But when Christ took on human form, God's kingdom, the kingdom of heaven, became eternally *present with* and *available to* us.

Undiscerning Christians (myself sometimes included) almost invariably think of God's kingdom and eternal life as for a much later time or in a place far removed from us. Nothing could be further from the truth, and nothing could leave us feeling more alone and hopeless when faced with the troubles of today.

If eternal life is not for the here and now, if God's kingdom is not both in and around us at this very moment, we have little more to cling to than a message of sin management. In this faux gospel, sin is presented as the primary problem, and accepting Jesus into our hearts is the cure.

But the gospel message Jesus actually proclaimed was, "Repent, for the kingdom of heaven [the kingdom of God] has come near"

(Matthew 3:2; 4:17, NRSV). Not near as in about to come, but near as in so close—offered to you through reliance on Jesus not merely as sin-deliverer but also as life-changer—that you can reach out and grab it at any moment.

"What must be emphasized in all of this," Willard wrote in *Divine Conspiracy*, "is the difference between trusting Christ, the real person Jesus, with all that that naturally involves, versus trusting some arrangement for sin-remission set up through him—trusting only His role as guilt remover. To trust the real person Jesus is to have confidence in him in every dimension of our real life, to believe that he is right about and adequate to everything," not just able to deal with our problems.[17]

Tragically, many Christians believe more in a God whose primary aim is to transfer credit from Christ's perfect account to ours, thus eradicating our debt of sin and giving us passage into heaven (mistakenly called "eternal life"). It's as if just by believing a certain theory about God's love and death on the cross—whether or not it changes any aspect of our life *today*, whether or not we trust God in the matters that concern us *here and now*—we "get saved." If this does not come dangerously close to salvation by works, it certainly skates on the thin ice of salvation by "right thinking" alone.

Discerning faith is more than just knowing the right doctrine. This will not be a surprising statement to many of you. However, it takes continuous discernment to tell if we are living an eternal life now, if we are trusting Jesus not merely as "guilt remover" but as Lord of our entire lives.

In John 5:39-40, Jesus spoke these incredibly challenging words: "You have your heads in your Bibles constantly because you think you'll find eternal life there. But you miss the forest for the trees. These Scriptures are all about *me*! And here I am, standing right before you, and you aren't willing to receive from me the life you say you want."

The life we yearn for, the life we say we want, is not just a life of "correct doctrine" but a life of vital and ongoing trust in who the Scriptures reveal.

Paying Close Attention to Reality

True discernment helps us apply these truths to our daily walk with God, including our devotions. It allows us to experience the Bible as what Martin Luther called a "Feuerzeug" (modern Germans use this word for a pocket lighter), a spark that ignites the fire of God within us.[18] How I long for on-fire times in the Scripture like Luther had! I don't want to have an encounter with some words on a page (no matter how wise or right they may be). I long for a heart-to-heart experience with the Source of these words, with Life Himself.

In *The Pursuit of God*, A. W. Tozer rightly noted that we often "read our chapter, have our short devotions and rush away, hoping to make up for our deep inward bankruptcy."[19] But Jesus' call to meditate on (to dwell on, ponder, and explore) His Word implies that God wants us to delight not in the Scriptures themselves but in *who* they reveal.

This practice may be referred to by the name *contemplation*, a term that suffers profound misunderstanding. Some Christians have never bothered to investigate this expression. Others (this is where I've most often fallen) have assumed they know what it means but have largely ignored it. And some relegate it to the life of mystics and monks. For them, contemplation matters little to the daily life of average Christians.

I appreciate the simple yet powerful way Dean Brackley defined contemplation in his book *The Call to Discernment in Troubled Times*. He expressed,

> *By contemplation, [I] mean paying close attention to reality and allowing the truth to sink in, penetrate us, and stir our feelings and*

thoughts. *We need contemplation in this sense the way we need food, water, and recreation, the way we need to brush our teeth and practice other daily disciplines. Without it, we fall into one of those unreflective lives that is hardly worth living.*[20]

All of us can benefit from paying closer attention to reality, from allowing the truth to genuinely change us. But contemplation requires a certain degree of intention and purpose that few of us consistently devote to our spiritual life. Perhaps this is why contemplation has been sequestered by many to monastery cloisters.

No matter how many days in a row I might carry on the practice of dribbling myself with a few drops of water, I would never get a cleansing shower. In the same way, to sprinkle a few verses or prayers on ourselves throughout the week will not accomplish the deep reordering of our minds, the transformation of our thinking, that actually ushers in the life we crave.

We will find that if we desire to be changed, we must rearrange our whole lives. How penetrating and difficult this truth is for me to live out: "One cannot tack an effective, life-transforming practice of prayer and study onto 'life as usual.' Life as usual must go. It will be replaced by something far better."[21]

I may not always like "life as usual," but I know it. It's comfortable and definitely more predictable than an untested and unknown existence, even if it promises to be "something far better." Ah, but here is the real issue: Most of the time we don't *really* believe that life surrendered to God will be what it promises. Discernment helps us see that it *is*.

A Life to Be Enjoyed . . .
This is how A. W. Tozer described Christianity. Not merely a "doctrine to be held" but "a life to be enjoyed."[22] You've got to love that.

But I'll tell you the problem I've had with living out this idea. I've often been so busy clenching my jaw in effort, trying *so hard* to do the "right thing," that I simply have not been able to enjoy the life of faith.

Through years of wrestling and learning to better discern His voice, I've discovered that one major reason for my former "teeth clenched until I'm holy" ways was that I spent all kinds of effort trying to change my *behavior*, when what really needed transformation was my inner being—the thoughts and beliefs that drove my actions.

When we spin our wheels in desperate attempts to change our lives, we can become disillusioned and frustrated with the promises of Scripture. We may begin to wonder if we'll ever *really* change. We start to think, *What's wrong with me? Why am I still struggling with the same old things (or new things more intensely)?*

I don't know about you, but I don't want to sit around feeling guilty, wondering if I'll ever live the life I'm "supposed to" live. I want God to change me, really change me. I yearn to *delight* in God.

But even when phrases from Scripture such as "turn the other cheek," "love your enemies," "be angry but do not sin," and "speak the truth in love" inspire longing in us to change, they may also move us to hopeless, shame-ridden resignation. And this despair would be absolutely spot-on; doing all the things Christ taught us to do would be absolutely impossible *if not for the power of God* changing us from the inside out. Without Him completely overhauling our minds, we could not do any of the marvelous and miraculous things God commands us to do.

Discernment helps us *determine* to pursue genuine inner transformation. This may sound simple, but it's not. (In fact, it may sound a lot like what many discouraged Christians have already tried.) Intending to be changed from the inside out involves doing away with "life as usual." It means investing time and energy in silence and solitude with

God. Only in silence and solitude can we hear God's voice calling us to a life of deeper faith and love than we've yet experienced. Intentional faith also involves taking our belief into the realm of action. We may know a lot of "right answers," but we don't truly believe them unless we consistently *act* as if they're true.

The point of knowing, of authentically believing, what Jesus said is not so that we can win Bible trivia games or even convert our non-Christian friends. The advantage in such life-changing belief is that we can actually deal with reality, with the storms and stresses that *will* come. Jesus Himself proclaimed,

> *These words I speak to you are not incidental additions to your life, homeowner improvements to your standard of living. They are foundational words, words to build a life on. If you work these words into your life, you are like a smart carpenter who built his house on solid rock. Rain poured down, the river flooded, a tornado hit — but nothing moved that house. It was fixed to the rock.*
>
> *But if you just use my words in Bible studies and don't work them into your life, you are like a [foolish] carpenter who built his house on the sandy beach. When a storm rolled in and the waves came up, it collapsed like a house of cards. (Matthew 7:24-27)*

Discerning faith acknowledges God's words as the foundation for the life we crave, the very source of life change. So as we close this chapter, I urge you to allow the Word of God to be fully integrated into your daily life. Let your thought life and the beliefs that compel you to act be tried and transformed by God. There are many excellent resources that can help you continue this journey.[23]

The choices we make about faith will unfold from now through eternity, shaping our entire lives from the inside out. Dear friends, let us go forth, armed and ready to grab hold of a life of discerning faith!

Questions for Discussion

1. Saint Thomas Aquinas remarked that "love . . . is born of an earnest consideration of the object loved."[24] Take some time to earnestly consider and discuss God, the object of all our love. How does the thought that God lives a very interesting and full life strike you? How do His attributes make you feel? What about the ways He has revealed Himself in your own life and in the lives of the other group members? As you keep your discussion focused on God, watch your adoration for Him grow.

2. Discuss or journal about the following idea: "God didn't die to save Mount Everest or the Tahitian sunset, as awesome as they might be. He died for individuals—broken or battered, mean or catty, abused or addicted—who He proclaims are capable of revealing and enjoying greater beauty and goodness than even the most sublime works of nature." How does the phrase "original glory" hit you? What challenges arise in believing that you—a beloved individual for whom Christ died—have an incomparable "original glory" and are able to reveal and enjoy more splendor than the most awesome spectacles of natural wonder?

3. What do you think of the idea that we cannot tack a life-transforming practice of prayer and Bible reading onto "life as usual"? What parts of you resist the claim that "life as usual must go"? In what ways is it difficult for you to believe that it will be replaced by something far better?

Thoughts for Personal Meditation

Would it be easy or difficult for you to refer to yourself, as John did, as "the disciple Jesus loved"? Are you certain there is no catch, no end to the goodness of God's love for you? What are some formative childhood experiences that may have influenced your answers? Explore the ways in which you may have poked loopholes in God's promises (yeah, yeah, yeah; God loves me, *but* . . .).

A Prayer to Spark Your Conversation with God

Holy God, only You can make the life I crave possible. Sheer muscle and willpower don't make anything happen. But every word You've spoken to me is a Spirit-word, and so it is life-giving and life-fulfilling. Still, some of me is resisting, refusing to grab hold of this truth. Help me, Lord, in my unbelief. I confess it to You and ask You to transform it. Grow my desire to truly believe, deep down to the core of who I am. Precious Father, You are both tender and kind, not easily angered, immense in love. You never, never quit. From the bottom of my heart, I thank You! Train me, God, to walk straight. Put me together, one heart and mind; then, undivided, I'll worship in joyful fear. In the almighty name of Jesus I pray, amen.[25]

Benediction

I RECOGNIZE THAT IN this book we've explored *a lot* of information. No one could recall it perfectly. So as particular situations unfold, I encourage you to return to specific chapters or to the general principles of discernment outlined throughout the book. I'd also like to leave you with some final practical tips for exercising discernment.

As you read, please remember that while these ideas can be applied to many situations, they are *not* one-size-fits-all formulas. When discerning the will of God, inclining yourself to the three lights—God's Spirit, the Bible, and your specific circumstances—will always remain of utmost importance.

With that said, might I suggest that in exercising discernment you keep these tips in mind:

- *Simplify.* Though many choices challenge us with confounding complexity, even the most complicated decisions can be broken down into smaller "yes or no" choices. This makes larger multifaceted choices a bit more manageable, removing the clutter so that we can see clearly (one of our definitions of discernment!) what's essential to the matters at hand.
- *Buy yourself time.* If you feel pressured to make a decision but are still unsure which alternative to choose, clear time in your schedule (lock yourself in the bathroom for ten minutes, cancel a meeting or a lunch with your friend, do whatever you have to do) to get mental and physical space.

- *Stay attuned to your emotions.* Because our feelings play an incredibly important part in good discernment, I've devoted an entire chapter to the matter. We explored earlier how to read the movements of consolation and desolation, as well as the role of indifference in wise decision making. This list would be incomplete, however, if I didn't reemphasize emotion's key role.
- *Mentally experiment with your options.* Journal, pray, and perhaps try one of the following experiments, developed in the sixteenth century by a master of discernment, Ignatius of Loyola:
  - ▶ Consider what you'd counsel a person you've never before met to choose if she described your current situation as her own. Suppose you wish only the best for this person and for the greater good of humanity.
  - ▶ Imagine you're on your deathbed. Consider what you'll wish then that you'd chosen now. Select that which will give you the same peace and satisfaction you'd want on your last earthly day.
  - ▶ Picture yourself meeting Christ after death and being asked to give an account of your decision in the current circumstance. Which choice would you find easier to reconcile with His justice and love?

Or try this experiment of Dallas Willard's: When a clear answer does not come while praying for God's direction, Willard recommends people devote the next couple of hours to something that neither engrosses their mental faculties nor focuses too intently on the matter in question (something like gardening, housework, or paying bills will do). This leaves the mind ready to receive an answer from God if He chooses to speak. In *Hearing God,* Willard wrote, "I have learned not to worry about whether or not this is going to work. I know that it does not have to work, but I am sure that it will work if God has something he really wants me to know or do. This is ultimately because I am sure of how great and good he is."[1]

- *Initially stick with one option at a time.* Although comparing alternatives is certainly helpful and important in making a wise decision, trouble often comes in constantly jumping back and forth between two options. In separately evaluating your choices, you may be able to better distinguish between the good and the better.

- *Seek the counsel of others.* In the timeless words of Proverbs 15:22, "Without counsel, plans go wrong, but with many advisers they succeed" (NRSV). It's always wise to bring at least two people whose walk with God you trust—people who will give you as objective and truthful counsel as possible—into any major decision. Preferably, these people should not be directly affected by or involved in the circumstances surrounding your choice.

- *Remember to include the "no."* In making any decision, you affirm one thing and deny a number of alternatives. When saying yes to a particular option, remember to say a firm mental and emotional no to the others. If we fail to do this, we may mistakenly lament the possibilities we didn't select, as if we once had them and no longer do. But this idea—that freedom means people should not have to close doors behind them after choosing to embark on a certain path—can be dangerous indeed. As scholar Dean Brackley reminded us, the reality is that "we may have a hundred dreams, but ninety-plus will have to die for one or two to become reality."[2] We frequently forget to acknowledge and grieve the choices we lose by exercising our freedom to decide. Oftentimes, we need to mourn rejected alternatives so that we can finally let them go and wholeheartedly embrace our chosen option.

- *Follow up.* If you feel God drawing you to something, but you don't have to make an immediate decision, commit to pursuing it further. Follow your inclinations with study, prayerful meditation, and/or a discussion of the possibilities with a mentor (to maintain objectivity, perhaps refrain initially from telling him or her what you think God may be leading you to do).
- *Evaluate the past and explore the future.* I appreciate the candid questions Pierre Wolff counseled people to ask in his book *Discernment*:

> *In which decisions did I undergo needless anxieties and worries just because I postponed my decision too long? Taking into account the degree of importance of a decision to come, how much time will I allow myself to make it? What values are implied in the choice I am considering right now? How do they match with mine? How will I safeguard my values by my choice?*[3]

Like the ancient process of examen, this pause to take stock of things can be done with any decision (or daily, as some church fathers recommended). Discerning minds review the past in order to choose wisely in the future.

- *Flex as things change.* Discernment helps us discover God's will for the present. But since the best course of action always depends on the particulars of a given situation, and situations change, we may be called to recognize that what once was the right or best choice no longer is. You may join a short-term mission team, for instance, and become too sick to go. This doesn't automatically mean that you made a poor or "wrong" decision. God may simply be calling you to flex with Him, discerning His unfolding will for today.

- *Rest in His goodness.* I love the startlingly confident words of Thomas à Kempis in *The Imitation of Christ*: "Do whatever lies in your power and God will assist your good intentions. Trust neither in your own knowledge nor in the cleverness of any human being; rather trust in God's grace."[4] We don't need to fear that God is waiting around to punish us for making bad choices. Our good Father doesn't want to trick or tease us. As you eagerly pursue His will, God will bless your right intentions. I counsel you, as Saint Augustine famously did, "Love God and do what you will."[5]

- *Mercilessly remove any hindrance to hearing God's voice.* As we've seen, the absence of a word from God regarding a particular decision doesn't automatically mean that you're in sin. But it certainly can. Again, trusting in His goodness, we can be sure that if we genuinely desire to know if something is hindering our communication with God, He will find a way to tell us. I suggest setting aside a specific length of time (even as much as a couple of days) to quietly listen for any indication that you're blocking His voice, believing that He will convict an authentically penitent heart. When you do this, one of two things might happen:

  ► You may sense that some sin has quenched the Spirit within you. If so, ruthlessly and completely eliminate whatever stands in the way of your communion with God. He promises, without condition, that "if we confess our sins, he will forgive our sins, because we can trust God to do what is right. He will cleanse us from all the wrongs we have done" (1 John 1:9, NCV).

  ► Or, even after a reasonable amount of time, God may remain silent on a particular matter. In that case, pursue the idea that there may be various things that would equally please God. Perhaps He doesn't desire at this time to direct you in one way or another. When I tell my daughters that they may play outside, they know there are many acceptable things they can do. I don't have to direct them specifically to ride their bikes or tend to their pet pill bug, Pilly. They may choose from any number of activities that would give both of them—and me—joy. A similar thing sometimes happens with God. His will may be that you decide.

God's will may be that you decide—today—to continue mining the riches of discernment. Our journey together has come to an end, but your adventures will continue, as will mine.

Indeed, because growing in discernment is a lifelong process, we can joyfully anticipate moving further along. As we do, I once again

ask—ask the God of our Master, Jesus Christ, the God of glory—to make you intelligent and discerning in knowing him personally, your eyes focused and clear, so that you can see exactly what it is he is calling you to do, grasp the immensity of this glorious way of life he has for his followers, oh, the utter extravagance of his work in us who trust him—endless energy, boundless strength! (Ephesians 1:17-19).

Endless energy, boundless strength, eyes focused and clear, grasping the glorious way of life He has for His followers—*this* is the life I crave.

What is the life *you* crave?

Notes

INTRODUCTION

1. Russ Johnston, *How to Know the Will of God* (Colorado Springs, CO: NavPress, 1971), 5.
2. Evelyn Underhill, *Abba: Meditations Based on the Lord's Prayer* in John F. Thornton and Susan B. Varenne, eds., *Practical Mysticism* and *Abba* (New York: Vintage Books, 2003), 149, emphasis added.
3. Pierre Wolff, *Discernment: The Art of Choosing Well: Based on Ignatian Spirituality*, 2nd ed. (Ligouri, MO: Ligouri/Triumph, 2003), 34.
4. Dallas Willard, *Hearing God: Developing a Conversational Relationship with God* (Downers Grove, IL: InterVarsity, 1999), 212, emphasis added.

CHAPTER 1: Discernment: *The Art of Living Well*

1. Gordon T. Smith, *The Voice of Jesus: Discernment, Prayer, and the Witness of the Spirit* (Downers Grove, IL: InterVarsity, 2003), 134.
2. Dallas Willard, *Hearing God: Developing a Conversational Relationship with God* (Colorado Springs, CO: NavPress, 2003), 194.
3. Dallas Willard, *Renovation of the Heart: Putting on the Character of Christ* (Colorado Springs, CO: NavPress, 2002), 90, 142.
4. For more on this idea, see Dallas Willard, *Hearing God*, 28.
5. Dr. Dan B. Allender and Dr. Tremper Longman III, *Bold Love* (Colorado Springs, CO: NavPress, 1992), 11.
6. Jerry Bridges, *The Pursuit of Holiness* (Colorado Springs, CO: NavPress, 2003), 22.
7. Martha Peace, *Damsels in Distress: Biblical Solutions for Problems Women Face* (Phillipsburg, NJ: P&R Publishing, 2006), 121.
8. E. Stanley Jones, "For Sunday of Week 41," *Victorious Living* (Nashville: Abingdon, 1938), 281.

9. J. I. Packer, *Knowing God* (Downers Grove, IL: InterVarsity, 1993), 103.

10. Portions of this paragraph have been adapted from Jerusha Clark, *Every Thought Captive: Battling the Toxic Beliefs That Separate Us from the Life We Crave* (Colorado Springs, CO: NavPress, 2006), 1–2.

11. Willard, *Renovation of the Heart*, 95.

12. Dallas Willard and Jan Johnson, *Renovation of the Heart in Daily Practice* (Colorado Springs, CO: NavPress, 2006), 77.

13. Smith, 25.

14. Willard, *Hearing God*, 58-59, emphasis added.

15. E. Stanley Jones, *A Song of Ascents* (Nashville: Abingdon, 1979), 190.

16. F. B. Meyer, *The Secret of Guidance: Guideposts for Life's Choices* (Chicago: Moody, 1997), 31.

17. Willard, *Hearing God*, 199.

18. Willard, *Hearing God*, 196.

19. Willard, *Hearing God*, 71.

20. For more on the ideas in this section, I recommend John Eldredge, *Waking the Dead: The Glory of a Heart Fully Alive* (Nashville: Thomas Nelson, 2003).

21. J. B. Philips, *God Our Contemporary* (New York: MacMillan, 1960), accessed online at www.religion-online.org, chapter 19.

22. Dr. Dan B. Allender and Dr. Tremper Longman III, *The Cry of the Soul: How Our Emotions Reveal Our Deepest Questions About God* (Colorado Springs, CO: NavPress, 1994), 243–245.

23. Phyllis Tickle, *The Shaping of a Life: A Spiritual Landscape* (New York: Image Books, 2003), 22–23.

24. Adapted from Daniel 2:20-21, MSG; Daniel 2:22-23, NCV; and Psalm 119:125,169, NLT.

CHAPTER 2: Emotional Discernment: *Finding the Still Point*

1. *Random House Webster's College Dictionary*, 2nd ed., s.v. "valid" and "validate."

2. Gordon T. Smith, *The Voice of Jesus: Discernment, Prayer, and the Witness of the Spirit* (Downers Grove, IL: InterVarsity, 2003), 56. For many of the thoughts in the following paragraphs I am

indebted to the illuminating discussion Smith presented throughout *The Voice of Jesus*.

3. From Smith's analysis of Wesley's work in *The Voice of Jesus*, 46.

4. Jonathan Edwards, *A Treatise Concerning Religious Affections (1746)*, in *The Works of Jonathan Edwards* (New Haven, CT: Yale University Press, 2003), 146.

5. Lewis B. Smedes, *Choices: Making Right Decisions in a Complex World* (New York: HarperCollins, 1991), 38.

6. Dallas Willard, *Renovation of the Heart: Putting on the Character of Christ* (Colorado Springs, CO: NavPress, 2002), 33.

7. Gerald O'Mahoney, *Finding the Still Point* (Surrey, England: Eagle, 1993), 9.

8. Pierre Wolff, trans., *The Spiritual Exercises of Saint Ignatius: A New Translation from the Authorized Latin Text* (Liguori, MO: Liguori/Triumph, 1997), paragraph 315.

9. Dean Brackley, *The Call to Discernment in Troubled Times: New Perspectives on the Transformative Wisdom of Ignatius of Loyola* (New York: Crossroad, 2004), 50.

10. Wolff, paragraph 179.

11. George E. Ganss, SJ, *The Spiritual Exercises of St. Ignatius* (St. Louis, MO: IJS, 1992), 151.

12. Brackley, 12.

13. Dr. Dan B. Allender and Dr. Tremper Longman III, *The Cry of the Soul: How Our Emotions Reveal Our Deepest Questions About God* (Colorado Springs, CO: NavPress, 1994), 150.

14. Adapted from Candy Paull, "When I Need Guidance," in *Everyday Prayers for Everyday Cares for Women* (Tulsa, OK: Honor Books, 2002), 92; Jeremiah 17:9-10, MSG.

CHAPTER 3: **Sex, Beauty, and the Figure You Crave:** *Discernment and Your Body*

1. If you're interested in reading more about body image and my particular struggle with it, see "Shaped: Living As God's Masterpiece," in *Every Thought Captive: Battling the Toxic Beliefs That Separate Us from the Life We Crave* (Colorado Springs, CO: NavPress, 2006), 153–177.

2. N. T. Wright, *Simply Christian: Why Christianity Makes Sense*

(New York: HarperOne, 2006), 64–65.

3. Paraphrase by Dallas Willard.

4. Dallas Willard, *Renovation of the Heart: Putting on the Character of Christ* (Colorado Springs, CO: NavPress, 2002), 159.

5. Evelyn Underhill, *Practical Mysticism: A Little Book for Normal People* (New York: E. P. Dutton & Company, 1928), 158.

6. Underhill, 164.

7. Allan Bloom, *The Closing of the American Mind* (New York: Touchstone, 1987), 67.

8. Karen Lee-Thorp and Cynthia Hicks, *Why Beauty Matters* (Colorado Springs, CO: NavPress, 1997), 17.

9. Naomi Wolf, *The Beauty Myth: How Images of Beauty Are Used Against Women* (New York: William Morrow, 1991), 52, emphasis added.

10. Mary Pipher, PhD, *Reviving Ophelia: Saving the Selves of Adolescent Girls* (New York: Penguin Group, Riverhead Trade Paperback Edition, 2005), 68.

11. B. J. Gallagher, *Everything I Need to Know I Learned from Other Women* (York Beach, ME: Cohari, 2002), 109, reported in Lee-Thorp and Hicks, 14.

12. Lee-Thorp and Hicks, 116.

13. Brennan Manning, *The Ragamuffin Gospel* (Sisters, OR: Multnomah, 2000), 88–89.

14. Wright, 40–41, 44.

15. William Gurnall, *The Christian in Complete Armour*, rev. ed., ed. James S. Bell Jr. (1655; repr., Lindale, TX: World Challenge, Inc., 1994), 11.

16. Lee-Thorp and Hicks, 30, emphasis added.

17. Lewis B. Smedes, *Sex for Christians: The Limits and Liberties of Sexual Living* (Grand Rapids, MI: Eerdmans, 1994), 3, 5.

18. Smedes, 145.

19. Smedes, 93.

20. Smedes, 212.

21. This idea is adapted from Wright, 232.

22. Jeff Pollard, *Christian Modesty and the Public Undressing of America* (San Antonio, TX: The Vision Forum, Inc., 2002), 21.

CHAPTER 4: **Stopping the Flow:** *How Discernment Transforms What You Say*

1. Martha Peace, *Damsels in Distress: Biblical Solutions for Problems Women Face* (Phillipsburg, NJ: P&R Publishing, 2006), 30.
2. Joseph Stowell, *The Weight of Your Words: Measuring the Impact of What You Say* (Chicago: Moody, 1998), 37.
3. Stowell, 138.
4. Peace, 35.
5. Stowell, 72.
6. Jean-Paul Sartre, *Being and Nothingness* (New York: Washington Square Press, 1984), 350.
7. Lewis B. Smedes, *Shame and Grace: Healing the Shame We Don't Deserve* (San Francisco: HarperSanFranciso, 1993), iii.
8. As told in Stowell, 18.
9. I've updated Underhill's words here. For the original, see Evelyn Underhill, *Abba: Meditations Based on the Lord's Prayer* in John F. Thornton and Susan B. Varenne, eds., *Practical Mysticism* and *Abba* (New York: Vintage Books, 2003), 160–161.
10. *Random House Webster's College Dictionary* (New York: Random House, 1997), s.v. "cynical."
11. *Random House Webster's College Dictionary.*
12. Martha Peace evaluated many of these manipulative ploys in her book *Damsels in Distress.* See page 61 for a helpful chart.
13. Peace, 65.
14. Stowell, 29.
15. Story recounted in Stowell, 36.

CHAPTER 5: **Beyond Distraction:** *Where Discernment and Your Resources Intersect*

1. Eugene H. Peterson, *A Long Obedience in the Same Direction: Discipleship in an Instant Society* (Downers Grove, IL: InterVarsity, 2000), 46.
2. Blaise Pascal, *Pensées*, 131. Quoted in Thomas Merton, *The Inner Experience: Notes on Contemplation* (New York: HarperCollins, 2003), 51.
3. Dallas Willard, *The Divine Conspiracy: Rediscovering Our Hidden*

Life in God (New York: HarperSanFrancisco, 1998), 324.

4. For an extraordinarily insightful discussion of this question, see Willard, 167-168.

5. Thomas à Kempis, "Sorrow of Heart," in *The Imitation of Christ*, trans. Harry Plantinga, accessed through Quick Verse 8.0 Deluxe, 1994.

6. Brother Lawrence, "Concerning Wandering Thoughts in Prayer," in *The Practice of the Presence of God* (Uhrichsville, OH: Barbour, 2004), 64.

7. François Fénelon, *Talking with God*, trans. Hal M. Helms (Brewster, MA: Paraclete Press, 1997), 74.

8. Fénelon, 76.

9. Fénelon, 75.

10. Ian P. McGreal, ed., *Great Thinkers of the Western World: The Major Ideas and Classic Works of More Than 100 Outstanding Western Philosophers, Physical and Social Scientists, Psychologists, Religious Writers and Theologians* (New York: HarperCollins, 1992), 93–94.

11. Jerry Bridges, *The Pursuit of Holiness* (Colorado Springs, CO: NavPress, 2003), 129.

12. Merton, 53.

13. Portions adapted from Psalm 19:7-8,11, MSG; and Psalm 19:14, NLT.

CHAPTER 6: **Your Divine Invitation:** *Exercising Vocational Discernment*

1. Gene Edward Veith Jr., *God at Work: Your Christian Vocation in All of Life* (Wheaton, IL: Crossway, 2002), 17.

2. Veith, 16.

3. Gustaf Wingren, *Luther on Vocation*, trans. Carl C. Rasmussen (Evansville, IN: Ballast Press, 1994), 6.

4. Douglas J. Schuurman, *Vocation: Discerning Our Callings in Life* (Grand Rapids, MI: Eerdmans, 2004), 123.

5. Wingren, 10.

6. Veith, 23–24.

7. Schuurman, 46.

8. Schuurman, xi, 3–4, 72.

9. Frederick Buechner, *Listening to Your Life: Daily Meditations with Frederick Buechner* (New York: HarperCollins, 1992), 186. In an interview for *Religion and Ethics Newsweekly*, Buechner continued, "The vocation for you is the one in which your deep gladness and the world's deep need meet. When you are doing what you are happiest doing, it must also be something that not only makes you happy but that the world needs to have done. In other words, if what makes you happy is going out and living it up and spending all your money on wine, women, and song, the world doesn't need that. But on the other hand, if you give your life to good works—you go and work in a leper colony and it doesn't make you happy—the chances are you're not doing it very well. Those for whom you were doing it will recognize that this is not an act of love. It's a good work and they are the object of it." Bob Abernethy, "Interview: Frederick Buechner," *Religion and Ethics Newsweekly*, April 5, 2006, http://www.pbs.org/wnet/religionandethics/week936/interview.html.

10. Schuurman, 160.

11. Dean Brackley, *The Call to Discernment in Troubled Times: New Perspectives on the Transformative Wisdom of Ignatius of Loyola* (New York: Crossroad, 2004), 59.

12. Veith, 15.

13. John Calvin, *Treatises Against the Anabaptists and Against the Libertines*, ed. and trans. Benjamin Wirt Farley (Grand Rapids, MI: Baker, 1988), 278.

14. Veith, 135.

15. Wingren, 121.

16. Thomas Merton, *The Inner Experience: Notes on Contemplation* (New York: HarperCollins, 2003), 138.

17. Saint John of the Cross, *Spiritual Canticle*, xxix, 3, as quoted in Merton, 100.

18. Dallas Willard, *The Divine Conspiracy: Rediscovering Our Hidden Life in God* (New York: HarperSanFrancisco, 1998), 358–360.

19. Martin Buber, *The Eclipse of God*, in Maurice S. Friedman, *Martin Buber: The Life of Dialogue* (New York: Routledge, 2002), 132, emphasis added.

20. Stefan Kiechle, *The Art of Discernment: Making Good Decisions in Your World of Choices* (Notre Dame, IN: Ave Maria Press, 2005), 54.

21. Gordon T. Smith, *The Voice of Jesus: Discernment, Prayer, and*

the *Witness of the Spirit* (Downers Grove, IL: InterVarsity, 2003), 188–189.

22. Kiechle, 50–51.

23. Adapted from Schuurman, 161.

24. William E. Diehl, *In Search of Faithfulness: Lessons from the Christian Community* (Philadelphia: Fortress, 1982), 38.

25. Saint John of the Cross, *Dark Night of the Soul*, trans. and ed. E. Allison Peers (New York: Image Books, 2005), 182.

26. Karl Barth, *Church Dogmatics: The Doctrine of Creation*, vol. 3, part 4, ed. G. W. Bromiley (Edinburgh, Scotland: T&T Clark, 1961), 606.

27. First sentence quoted from François Fénelon, *Fénelon: Meditations on the Heart of God*, trans. Robert J. Edmonson (Brewster, MA: Paraclete Press, 1997), 40. Second portion adapted from Evelyn Underhill, *Practical Mysticism* and *Abba*, eds. John F. Thornton and Susan B. Varenne (New York: Vintage Books, 2003), 40.

CHAPTER 7: **Relationships Are Messy:** *Discernment Is Necessary*

1. Stefan Kiechle, *The Art of Discernment: Making Good Decisions in Your World of Choices* (Notre Dame, IN: Ave Maria Press, 2005), 35.

2. Evelyn Underhill, *Practical Mysticism* and *Abba*, eds. John F. Thornton and Susan B. Varenne (New York: Vintage Books, 2003), 206.

3. Philip Yancey, *What's So Amazing About Grace?* (Grand Rapids, MI: Zondervan, 1997), 62, 104.

4. Gerald O'Mahoney, *Abba! Father!* (Middlegreen, England: St. Paul Publications, 1987), 34, emphasis added.

5. Explained in Yancey, 96.

6. Underhill, 205.

7. Dr. Dan B. Allender and Dr. Tremper Longman III, *Bold Love* (Colorado Springs, CO: NavPress, 1992), 88, 90–91, emphasis added.

8. Allender and Longman, 92.

9. Allender and Longman, 162.

10. Eugene H. Peterson, *A Long Obedience in the Same Direction:*

Discipleship in an Instant Society (Downers Grove, IL: InterVarsity, 2000), 103.

11. Yancey, 175.

12. Frank Charles Laubach, *Man of Prayer: Selected Writings of a World Missionary* (Syracuse, NY: Laubach Literacy International, 1990), 154.

13. O'Mahoney, 37, 41.

14. Gordon MacDonald, quoted in Yancey, 15.

15. Dallas Willard, *Renovation of the Heart: Putting on the Character of Christ* (Colorado Springs, CO: NavPress, 2002), 264.

16. Allender and Longman, 211.

17. Lewis B. Smedes, *Sex for Christians: The Limits and Liberties of Sexual Living* (Grand Rapids, MI: Eerdmans, 1994), 126.

18. Thomas Merton, *The Inner Experience: Notes on Contemplation* (New York: HarperCollins, 2003), 144.

19. Adapted from Smedes, 128.

20. Dallas Willard, *The Divine Conspiracy: Rediscovering Our Hidden Life in God* (New York: HarperSanFrancisco, 1998), 231.

21. Willard, *The Divine Conspiracy*, 231.

22. Dr. Emerson Eggerichs, *Love & Respect: The Love She Most Desires; The Respect He Desperately Needs* (Brentwood, TN: Integrity, 2004), 158.

23. Portions adapted from Candy Paull, *Everyday Prayers for Everyday Cares for Women* (Tulsa, OK: Honor Books, 2002), 124.

CHAPTER 8: The Church: *Discerning Your Role in the Body of Christ*

1. Evelyn Underhill, *Abba: Meditations Based on the Lord's Prayer* in John F. Thornton and Susan B. Varenne, eds., *Practical Mysticism and Abba* (New York: Vintage Books, 2003), 173–174.

2. Ray C. Stedman, *Body Life: The Church Comes Alive* (Glendale CA: Regal, 1972), 13.

3. N. T. Wright, *Simply Christian: Why Christianity Makes Sense* (New York: HarperOne, 2006), 203–204.

4. This quote is attributed to Morton Kelsey by Brennan Manning in *The Ragamuffin Gospel* (Sisters, OR: Multnomah, 2000), 24, but no primary source citation is given. Since it has also been

attributed to a number of other individuals online (also without citation), I have not marked it as a direct quotation.

5. Henri J. M. Nouwen, *Out of Solitude: Three Meditations on the Christian Life* (Notre Dame, IN: Ave Maria Press, 1974), 23.

6. On this matter, I completely agree with N. T. Wright, who makes similar statements in *Simply Christian*, 123.

7. For some thoughts in this section, I am indebted to Skye Jethani's research for "iChurch: All We Like Sheep," *Leadership Journal* (Carol Stream, IL: Christianity Today International, Summer 2006).

8. Skye Jethani, "iChurch: All We Like Sheep." This article originally appeared in the Summer 2006 issue of *Leadership Journal*.

9. Roger Finke and Rodney Stark, *The Churching of America* (Chapel Hill, NC: Rutgers University Press, 1992), 17-21.

10. Jethani.

11. Christian Smith and Melinda Lundquist Denton, *Soul Searching: The Religious and Spiritual Lives of American Teenagers* (New York: Oxford University Press, 2005), 164–165.

12. Joseph Stowell, *The Weight of Your Words: Measuring the Impact of What You Say* (Chicago: Moody, 1998), 59.

13. Manning, 230–231.

14. Manning, 45–46.

15. Quoted here is a paraphrase by Brennan Manning, 46. You can read Maritain's original statements in Jacques Maritain, *The Degrees of Knowledge*, trans. G. B. Phelan (1932; repr., New York: Charles Scribner's Sons, 1959), 253.

16. Gordon T. Smith, *The Voice of Jesus: Discernment, Prayer, and the Witness of the Spirit* (Downers Grove, IL: InterVarsity, 2003), 176.

17. Stowell, 59.

18. "For the Church," prayer #7 in The Book of Common Prayer (1789; repr., New York: Oxford University Press, 1990), 816.

CHAPTER 9: Discerning Faith: *A Life to Be Enjoyed*

1. A. W. Tozer, *The Knowledge of the Holy: The Attributes of God: Their Meaning in the Christian Life* (New York: Harper and Brothers, 1961), 10.

2. Gerald O'Mahoney, *Abba! Father!* (Middlegreen, England: St. Paul Publications, 1987), 5.

3. Dallas Willard, *The Divine Conspiracy: Rediscovering Our Hidden Life in God* (New York: HarperSanFrancisco, 1998), 64.

4. Willard, *The Divine Conspiracy*, xiii.

5. Though I have footnoted only direct quotations from Willard's book, I would like to acknowledge my indebtedness to his work for helping me comprehend the ideas I discuss in the following several paragraphs.

6. Willard, *The Divine Conspiracy*, 63.

7. Brennan Manning, *The Ragamuffin Gospel* (Sisters, OR: Multnomah, 2000), 17–18.

8. Dallas Willard, *Renovation of the Heart: Putting on the Character of Christ* (Colorado Springs, CO: NavPress, 2002), 46.

9. John Eldredge, *Waking the Dead* (Nashville: Nelson, 2003), 14.

10. Henri J. M. Nouwen, *Life of the Beloved: Spiritual Living in a Secular World* (New York: Crossroad, 1992), 21.

11. G. K. Chesterton, "The Quick One," in *The Complete Father Brown* (West Valley City, UT: Waking Lion Press, 2006), 383. "It's so easy to be misunderstood," says Chesterton's character, Father Brown. "All men matter. You matter. I matter. It's the hardest thing in theology to believe."

12. Evelyn Underhill, *Abba: Meditations Based on the Lord's Prayer* in John F. Thornton and Susan B. Varenne, eds., *Practical Mysticism and Abba* (New York: Vintage Books, 2003), 161.

13. Dr. James Dobson, *Emotions: Can You Trust Them?* (Ventura, CA: Regal, 2003), 29–30.

14. Pierre Wolff, *Discernment: The Art of Choosing Well: Based on Ignatian Spirituality*, 2nd ed. (Ligouri, MO: Ligouri/Triumph, 2003), 120.

15. Quoted in Manning, 117.

16. Once again, though I have footnoted only direct quotations from Willard's book *The Divine Conspiracy*, I would like to acknowledge my indebtedness to his work for helping me comprehend the ideas I discuss in this section.

17. Willard, *The Divine Conspiracy*, 48–49.

18. Reported in Willard, *The Divine Conspiracy*, 256.

19. A. W. Tozer, *The Pursuit of God: The Human Thirst for the Divine,*

Tozer Legacy Edition (Camp Hill, PA: Christian Publications, Inc., 1982), 69.

20. Dean Brackley, *The Call to Discernment in Troubled Times: New Perspectives on the Transformative Wisdom of Ignatius of Loyola* (New York: Crossroad, 2004), 225.
21. Willard, *The Divine Conspiracy*, 356.
22. Tozer, *The Pursuit of God*, 36.
23. I've spent years of my own life devoted to these topics, and if you so desire, you can read some of what God taught me in *Every Thought Captive: Battling the Toxic Beliefs That Separate Us from the Life We Crave* (Colorado Springs, CO: NavPress, 2006).
24. Thomas Aquinas, *Summa Theologica*, translated by Fathers of the English Dominican Province, 1920. Published online by Kevin Knight of New Advent, www.newadvent.org.
25. Portions adapted from John 6:63-64, MSG; and Psalm 86:11-12,15, MSG.

BENEDICTION

1. Dallas Willard, *Hearing God: Developing a Conversational Relationship with God* (Downers Grove, IL: InterVarsity, 1999), 200.
2. Dean Brackley, *The Call to Discernment in Troubled Times: New Perspectives on the Transformative Wisdom of Ignatius of Loyola* (New York: Crossroad, 2004), 64.
3. Pierre Wolff, *Discernment: The Art of Choosing Well: Based on Ignatian Spirituality*, 2nd ed. (Ligouri, MO: Ligouri/Triumph, 2003), 16–17.
4. Thomas à Kempis, "Avoiding False Hope and Pride," in *The Imitation of Christ*, ed. and trans. Joseph N. Tylenda, SJ (New York: Vintage Books, 1998), 10.
5. Saint Augustine of Hippo, *In epistulam Ioannis ad Parthos* or *Homily 7 on the First Epistle of John*, trans. Kevin Knight, http://www.newadvent.org/fathers/170207.htm (accessed March 5, 2007).

About the Author

JERUSHA CLARK is the author of *Every Thought Captive* and *Inside a Cutter's Mind* and the coauthor of four other books, including the best seller *I Gave Dating a Chance*. She's passionate about ministering to people and wrestling with the questions closest to their hearts. Jerusha resides in Escondido, California, with her husband, Jeramy, a pastor at Emmanuel Faith Community Church, and her daughters, Jocelyn and Jasmine.